W9-BDU-231

PROFESSIONAL DEVELOPMENT AND PRACTICE SERIES
Ann Lieberman, *Editor*

Editorial Advisory Board: Myrna Cooper, Nathalie Gehrke,
Gary Griffin, Judith Warren Little, Lynne Miller,
Phillip Schlechty, Gary Sykes

Building a Professional Culture in Schools
Ann Lieberman, Editor

The Contexts of Teaching in Secondary Schools: Teachers' Realities
Milbrey W. McLaughlin, Joan E. Talbert,
and Nina Bascia, Editors

Careers in the Classroom: When Teaching Is More Than a Job
Sylvia Mei-Ling Yee

The Making of a Teacher: Teacher Knowledge and Teacher Education
Pamela L. Grossman

*Staff Development for Education in the 1990s:
New Demands, New Realities, New Perspectives,* SECOND EDITION
Ann Lieberman and Lynne Miller, Editors

*Teachers Who Lead: The Rhetoric of Reform and
the Realities of Practice*
Patricia A. Wasley

Exploring Teaching: Reinventing an Introductory Course
Sharon Feiman-Nemser and Helen J. Featherstone, Editors

Teaching: Making Sense of an Uncertain Craft
Joseph P. McDonald

Teachers' Work: Individuals, Colleagues, and Contexts
Judith Warren Little and Milbrey W. McLaughlin, Editors

Team Building for School Change: Equipping Teachers for New Roles
Gene I. Maeroff

A Union of Professionals: Labor Relations and Educational Reform
Charles Taylor Kerchner and Julia E. Koppich
in association with William Ayers, Krista D. Caufman,
Anthony M. Cresswell, James J. Gallagher, Byron King, Perry Lanier,
LeRae Phillips, and Mark A. Smylie

Team Building for School Change

Equipping Teachers for New Roles

Gene I. Maeroff

Teachers College, Columbia University
New York and London

Published by Teachers College Press, 1234 Amsterdam Avenue, New York, N.Y.
10027

Library of Congress Cataloging-in-Publication Data

Maeroff, Gene I.
    Team building for school change: equipping teachers for new roles
/Gene I. Maeroff.
        p.   cm.—(Professional development and practice series)
    Includes bibliographical references (p.) and index.
    ISBN 0-8077-3268-0 (alk. paper).—ISBN 0-8077-3267-2 (pbk.:
alk. paper)
    1. Teaching teams—United States. 2. Teachers—United States.
3. Educational change—United States. I. Title. II. Series.
LB1029.T4M34   1993
371.1'48—dc20   93-19983

ISBN 0-8077-3268-0
ISBN 0-8077-3267-2 (pbk.)

Printed on acid-free paper
Manufactured in the United States of America
99 98 97 96 95 94 93   8 7 6 5 4 3 2 1

FROM THE SERIES EDITOR

The central task of the current reform movement in education is nothing less than building and transforming schools that are struggling to achieve democratic ideals. The purpose of the *Professional Development and Practice Series* is to contribute to this historic transformation by presenting a variety of descriptions of practice-oriented research—narratives, stories, cases of innovative work—that can lead to a deeper understanding of educational practice and how to improve it. At this time of important educational change, we need to be informed by the special knowledge of university- and school-based educators who are working in and with the schools to illuminate how and in what ways positive change can take place.

As new organizational arrangements and collaborative relationships are being forged and studied, old, enduring problems are being looked at in new ways that are leading us to fresh insights. For example, the connections between teaching, learning, and assessment are being reexamined, and views of how teachers and students develop and learn are increasingly oriented toward those that involve the active participation of teachers and students in their own constructions of knowledge. The writers in this series are attempting to involve us in a dialogue about action, participation, and change based on the best evidence. They have undertaken to struggle with the problems of practice and the challenge of rethinking the future of our nation's schools.

While focusing on teacher teams and their use as a lever for change, Gene Maeroff also examines the importance of teachers becoming knowledgeable and skilled, and increasingly articulate about their leadership and participation so that they may take their rightful place in the school reform movement.

Maeroff has observed a variety of reform efforts that involved teams at the center of the change process. In this book he examines closely those sponsored by the Rockefeller Foundation, in which volunteer teams of teachers, learning how to lead the change process, were a primary intervention for professional development and eventual school change. Maeroff teaches us *why* teams can be an important vehicle, *how* they work and appear in different contexts, *what* serves as the content and process of their deliberations, as well as *where* they go wrong and *when* they go right.

Ann Lieberman

CONTENTS

FOREWORD

Gene Maeroff and I first met a dozen years ago. We were both with the *New York Times,* he as a veteran education writer and I as a fledgling editorialist. Having inherited the education beat on the editorial board from Fred Hechinger, I regularly sought out Gene as a source of news, trends, and insights in the field. He was then what he is today: a wise observer of the education scene who blends concern for America's schools with compassion for its children. Gene subsequently moved to the Carnegie Foundation for the Advancement of Teaching and I, after a stint in public television, to the Rockefeller Foundation to oversee its efforts in school reform.

In late 1989, the Rockefeller Foundation funded several new initiatives to help improve public schools that served poor and minority youngsters. One such program aimed at equipping teams of principals and teachers from schools to function as catalysts for change. We noted at the time that the distinct needs of inner-city youths and the unique circumstances of urban schools had changed remarkably in the last generation but that the preparation of educators for these schools was by and large caught in a time warp.

Michigan State University, under former Dean Judith Lanier, and the University of New Mexico, under erstwhile Dean David Colton, expressed interest in launching summer academies that would provide an immersion experience for school teams. Preliminary plans called for the academies to cover such subjects as:

- The roles of teachers and principals as catalysts for change
- Techniques of team building and school-based management
- Child development theory
- Recent research on effective instructional technique for at-risk youth
- Techniques for engaging parents in the educational enterprise

Our thought back then was that if the academies proved to be a powerful intervention, they would be sustained and replicated at public expense. We also hoped that if demonstrably successful, the academies would be positioned as something that progressive schools of education must offer and caring school districts must utilize. Lastly, they might serve as an opening wedge for reconceptualizing the traditional certification programs for principals and for reforming the basic education of teachers.

Cognizant of the fact that the Rockefeller Foundation had helped conceive the academies, we felt the need for an arm's-length observer to monitor their progress. We turned almost instinctively to Gene Maeroff, with his keen journalistic eye. Employed as a consultant by the foundation, he sat in on the summer academies, made follow-up visits to participating schools, and interviewed key players. Once embarked on this assignment, he conceived of this book, which would examine myriad efforts to build school-based teams and would assess the implications of this approach for broader school reform.

This book is about several programs as opposed to one and about works in progress rather than proven interventions. As with any endeavor that involves human beings and social institutions, both of which are complex and unpredictable, the assumptions with which one begins often bear only passing resemblance to reality as it unfolds. The key, from any foundation's perspective, is to encourage bright, caring people to dare, to dream, to explore, to experiment, to learn, and to share. The voyage is well worth the investment, even if the ultimate destination is somewhat different from that intended. Such has surely been the case with the academies funded by the Rockefeller Foundation—and, I suspect, with the other team building initiatives examined here. Cumulatively, these endeavors are steadily adding to the store of knowledge about what it takes to change schools for the benefit of children.

Our starting assumptions—for example, about the sustainability of academies with public support—may prove naive given the horrific fiscal pressures on school districts and public higher education. Even so, the academies have served as laboratories, insulated from the distractions of daily school life, where educators from schools and schools of education work closely together, often for the first time, on a curriculum and the process of professional development. The educators involved in the Rockefeller academies are on a learning curve. The jury is still out on the effectiveness of the academy experience and on the ultimate impact on the schools to which the teams return. Nevertheless, the academies in New Mexico and Michigan have already proven promising enough that they are spawning spin-off activities with the participating schools and even at the district and state levels.

Why this emphasis on the seemingly unexotic work of team building? Let's scan briefly the recent course of school reform. Barely over a decade ago, there was deep skepticism that public schools could do much to improve the life prospects of poor, minority children. Socioeconomic status, a proxy for the adequacy of family support, was deemed to be the determining factor. James Coleman's (1966) bleak prognosis for the impact of public schooling on disadvantaged children cast a pall over discussions about improving their academic performance. Those who refused to accept Coleman's thesis had little with which to rebut him beyond an abiding faith that poor children and inner-city schools weren't lost causes. The malaise among believers in public education was especially unsettling because of the assault by the incoming Reagan administration on federal funding for public schools.

To the rescue came Ronald Edmonds with his early research on effective schools. Although flawed, as any initial attempt invariably is, Edmonds' work at least offered some evidence—and thus hope—that children from all socioeconomic backgrounds are educable and that schools can be organized effectively to teach them. Confirming evidence surfaced at about the same time in a study of inner-city London schools, conducted by Michael Rutter and his colleagues (1979), entitled *15,000 Hours*. The research on effective schools helped transform the conversation about urban education from a discussion of whether inner-city schools were even salvageable to a search for ways to turn them around to improve outcomes for poor children. These preliminary breakthroughs helped spawn a decade of experimentation and action research aimed at uncovering interventions that might well make a difference.

The investments have borne impressive fruit, as is evidenced by the highly regarded work of the likes of James Comer, Ted Sizer, Howard Gardner, Henry Levin, and Bob Slavin, not to mention the scores of principals, teachers, superintendents, and education intermediaries who have made things markedly better for children.

Nevertheless, this work by and large goes on in nooks and crannies of schools and in classrooms here and there but does not permeate entire buildings, much less districts. These heroic reform efforts notwithstanding, teachers and teaching as a whole have not changed. The issue at this stage of the reform movement is how to move innovation from the incubator to widespread practice. What are the externalities and internal obstacles to systemic reform in entire buildings and districts, and how can they be surmounted? How, short of an epiphanic conversion, can enough teachers be reached so that entire schools are eventually transformed and, along with them, entire districts?

Frustrated reformers are these days groping for the levers of buildingwide change. What combination of interventions and circumstances, short of a burst of enlightenment or blowing up of the system, will spur educators to change? How do we energize educators to embrace a genuine reform agenda and enable entire faculties to pursue it on behalf of all children? This is a tall order because it entails altering deeply rooted perceptions and long-ingrained practices. Educators must undo what they've learned both about their professions and about their children. They must revisit assumptions about the capabilities of poor and minority children. If they do not, then as Lester

Thurow (1992) argues in *Head to Head,* society as a whole will suffer.

Many external forces impede reform, among them budget constraints, societal indifference, and excessive oversight. What's more, classroom teachers are among the most isolated of professionals. They desperately need exposure to new ideas, time to experiment, and encouragement to take risks. Yet, external regulations and standardized tests, which often dictate instruction, act as powerful disincentives to reform. To make matters worse, the paltry investments by school districts in professional development mean teachers have scant time for reflection and revitalization.

In this book, Gene Maeroff tells of the search for one lever for systemic change. Team building for cadres of school-based educators is intended to unleash well-informed, highly motivated change agents. As Maeroff observes, the idea of team building adheres to modern theories of participatory management articulated by the likes of W. Edwards Deming and Peter Drucker, among others. The keys, he finds, are perpetual intellectual and spiritual renewal, openness to change, and willingness to take risks. In other words, school must be a continuous learning environment for teachers as well as students.

Eschewing any abstract description or superficial analysis, Maeroff goes deep inside the team building programs to describe the nitty-gritty dynamics, tensions, and dilemmas. He provides a finely textured sense, for example, of what transpires in the summer academies and later on at school. One reads blow-by-blow descriptions of the impediments at the academy sites and the barriers encountered back home. He details how team building works, down to the designation of note takers, and conveys the teacher-to-teacher and teacher-to-principal dynamics.

Maeroff concludes, encouragingly, that the team building experiences are powerful. But they leave unanswered the question of how to engage the remaining faculty at home. There's little question that team building energizes those who participate. But the batteries invariably run down. What is required to keep them charged? Some team members are viewed upon reentry as elitists or are greeted with indifference. How can the predictable skepticism of nonparticipants be overcome? And skepticism isn't confined to the school itself. It extends to other layers of governance that influence school climate and practice. What then must be done to and for senior administrators, superintendents, school board members, legislators, and state education officials so that they advance rather than impede reform?

To his credit, Maeroff is not seduced by the enthusiasm of the participants. He is insightful about what has been learned and instructive about what we don't know. He asks penetrating questions about the effectiveness of teams and, thus, about their effects on overall reform. What are the limits of team building and building-based teams? Is a team even the right unit for initiating change? What must invariably be left to the entire faculty? What evidence is there, he asks, that working through teams is more effective that working through entire faculties?

Maeroff argues, quite accurately, that for the type of professional development embodied in team building to infuse the entire faculty, the schedules of schools must be reconstituted, district staff development budgets must be reconceptualized, and regulatory policies that constrain flexibility and experimentation must be relaxed. Much of this requires the school district's blessings. Can districts realistically be expected to foster serious professional development, he wonders, when their bureaucracies so typically stifle reform? Is reformist energy injected from the outside likely to spread if it depends, as it must, on the school bureaucracy to do so? That is the dilemma which has stalled systemic reform to date. Reform tends not to arise from inside, but it cannot possibly go to scale unless at some point it is internalized.

In effect, Gene Maeroff peers over the horizon toward the next frontier in school reform: sustained professional development for building-based educators. For all the promising experimentation and enlightened regulation, we simply cannot get from here to there without those who are responsible for teaching the children. Nor can they be expected to reconceive their practice in isolation or to wage war individually for change. This book graphically underscores the need to take professional development seriously if there is ever to be systematic reform.

Yet, staff development is a prime target in local fiscal crises. As it is so inadequate to begin with, it has proven to be easy pickings for budget cutters. Somewhere between the extremes of concentrated summer immersion experiences, such as academies, and desultory lectures on superintendents' days off, there waits to be designed and adopted a state-of-the-art approach to professional development that will spur genuine reform.

Ideally, professional development should consume a significant portion of a teacher's life. That's the case in Japan, where much of the teacher's time is spent outside the classroom. Consider the fact that in public school we expect every subject to be taught every day but that in college two or three sessions per week suffice for quality instruction. Custodial considerations aside, wouldn't several well-taught sessions of history each week be better for students than five badly taught ones?

As the enthusiasm of beneficiaries of team building indicates, educators desperately need time to be professionals. As the Iowa State Education Association put it in a report entitled *Time for Change* (n.d.), teachers need:

- time to educate every child fully;
- time for team planning, team teaching, and cooperative education at the building level;
- time to plan for comprehensive school change through participatory decision making;
- time to learn about and deploy new technologies that improve teaching and boost productivity for students and teachers;
- the redesign of instructional time to include a wider variety of teaching strategies, such as discovery and guided discovery, so that teaching styles can be matched with learning styles;
- relief from distracting intrusions into both instructional time and the learning environment. (p. 3)

Gene Maeroff clearly recognizes how crucial time is to systemic reform. Indeed, he devotes an entire chapter to this pivotal issue and goes so far as to suggest imaginative ways in which time in the school day can be freed up and then filled productively.

Enlightened corporations take professional development for granted. Those that are determined to be competitive invest heavily in people as well as technology. The hotel industry in this country would probably collapse if corporations zeroed out their training budgets. Companies that have adjusted successfully to new realities know that change is painstaking, time-consuming, and expensive. They even go through recognizable cycles of denying and then acknowledging the problem, followed by trashing and then training their employees. Sound familiar? The school reform movement stands at the brink of phase-4 training, having worked its way over the past dozen years through the first three. The prospect of shrinking market shares and profit margins drives corporations to respond. Ironically, it may take the threat of school vouchers and Whittle schools to quicken the pace of public school reform.

Although team building is by no means the answer, it does appear to be a promising way to jump-start reform. As Maeroff points out, team building utilizes the processes and embraces underlying principles that are integral to effective professional development. It is essential to instill within entire schools the kind of climate that team building at its best strives to create.

Maeroff's focus on building-based teams raises the question, however, of what else is needed if the reformist impulses unleashed are eventually to take hold. Given all the forces that impinge on life in the school building, it may well be necessary to implement vertically as well as horizontally integrated approaches to professional development. School-based personnel obviously need to be engaged in sustained, soundly conceived professional development activities. But others need to be awakened and sensitized as well. A presentation here or a lecture there will not do the trick for, say, unenlightened school board members. Brief but intense immersion experiences may also be indicated for governors, chief education officers, key legislators and their staffs, school board members, journalists, superintendents and senior administrators, parents' groups, and local business leaders—all of whose views and actions bear importantly on school expectations, perceptions, policies, and regulations. Finally, schools of education, which feed ill-prepared teachers into local districts, need to become state-of-the-art as well.

Although Gene Maeroff deftly uses a modest, admittedly unproven intervention as a point of departure, his book quite provocatively and usefully lifts the lid on a larger discussion of professional development that is long overdue. How do we foster systemic school reform in this country? What investments in the people who must do it are needed for it to be done? In our infatuation with innovation and our impatience with the pace of change, we have conveniently overlooked this central issue. Until we engage it forthrightly and imaginatively, as Gene Maeroff challenges us to do, the dream of systemic school reform will remain just that: a dream.

Hugh B. Price
Vice President
The Rockefeller Foundation

PREFACE

I am grateful to the Rockefeller Foundation for making it possible for me to write this book. The support I received from the foundation and the access I was given to the Leadership Academies that it funded provided the basis for my investigation of team building. This was the second time that I had the opportunity to observe a Rockefeller project over an extended period. My first working association with the foundation came in the mid-1980s, when I followed the progress of a national program that it sponsored for bolstering the teaching of humanities in secondary schools. My work at that time, which Rockefeller also supported, culminated in the publication of *The Empowerment of Teachers: Overcoming the Crisis of Confidence* in 1988.

This time around, I was invited by Hugh Price, a vice president of Rockefeller and a former colleague at the *New York Times,* to keep an eye on a new effort that the foundation was making to help improve elementary and secondary schools by conducting summer academies for teams of teachers. I wrote internal reports on the project for the foundation, reflecting on my experiences at the academies and on my visits to participating schools. As in my earlier work, I was free to make whatever other use I wished of my studies, and I was under no obligation whatsoever to assume any particular stance.

At the outset, it was unclear where the project would take me. I did not begin with the thought of focusing on team building. I didn't even know if my work would lead to a book on any topic. The idea of this book evolved as I tried to understand what was distinctive about the Leadership Academies and what their main contribution to school improvement might be.

After I seized on the theme of team building, I widened my field of inquiry. I discovered that other ventures into team building were being carried out on behalf of schools by other sponsors. As so often happens, various people and organizations—working independently of each other and frequently unknown to each other—were embarked on somewhat similar paths. It became clear that it would be worthwhile to pull together the lessons that were being learned. Adding to the appeal of the topic was the fact that team building is already the subject of a good deal of attention in business and industry.

It quickly grew obvious that the business model of team building, although relevant to schools, could not serve simply as a template. To whatever extent team building is useful in elementary and secondary education, it will be as a result of an approach that takes cognizance of the uniqueness of school teaching and of conditions in schools. The mission of changing children's lives cannot possibly be equated to the goal of accumulating larger profits.

Above all, team building in the educational arena has to be about helping teachers to improve as professionals. Most kinds of in-service have not been terribly effective in this regard, and something better is needed. Furthermore, enhanced professionalism among educators at this point in the nation's history has to mean being equipped to help bring about changes on behalf of students. There is such wide dissatisfaction with the ways in which elementary and secondary schools are now operating that the most important reason why teachers should raise their level of professionalism is that they will be more knowledgeable about educational change and more qualified to implement it. Thus, there is in this book the very natural merger of two ideas that come together in a synergistic manner: team building and school change.

Writing a book of this sort requires the cooperation of many people. I spent time at the academies for team building, where I circulated among the teams, participated with them in sessions, and observed interactions among members of the teams. When I went to the schools, I asked members of the school community—both those who had attended the academy and those who had not—many questions about the impact of team building on the schools.

In almost 30 years of doing this sort of work in schools, I am repeatedly impressed by the openness that I encounter. Yes, there are initial suspicions in some instances, but invariably these fade and I am able to gain the access that I need to do the job that I set out to do. Teachers—and principals, too, I might add—have jobs that are among the most difficult in this troubled society of ours. Yet, for the most part, they tend to be willing to open themselves to the scrutiny of writers and researchers.

I thank the many teachers and principals who trusted me so that I might carry out this project. In particular, I want to acknowledge the teachers and principals in New Mexico and Michigan—the two states in which my work was mainly concentrated—who were gracious and always accommodating during the visits I made, first to the academies and then to their schools.

I also could not have have written this book without the cooperation of people at the two universities that administered the grants for the Leadership Academies. At the University of New Mexico, I owe my gratitude to David Colton, Roberta Smith, and Mary Nordhaus. I can't say enough to thank them for their endless kindnesses, as well as for the many delicious Southwestern dinners we shared. At Michigan State

University, help and hospitality were extended to me at various points by Judith Lanier, Charles Thompson, Chester Francke, and Barbara Markle. They were candid and responsive to my requests. The aforementioned educators at the two universities were my primary contacts for this book during a period that extended over more than two years.

In attempting to widen the focus of the book, I was assisted by key people from the various programs on which I obtained information to supplement the data I had gathered on the Leadership Academies. In this regard, I was helped by Myra Cline and John Watkins of the Trek of the Coalition of Essential Schools, Brenda LeTendre of Accelerated Schools, Mary Lillesve of the Minnesota Educational Effectiveness Program, Sophie Sa and Kenneth Tewel of the Panasonic Foundation, Peggy Funkhouser of the Los Angeles Educational Partnership, Jean Adenika of the California Achievement Council, Ruth Whitman Chacon of the American Federation of Teachers, and Robert McClure of the National Education Association.

There is a rich and lively literature that did much to inform my work. The articles, books, and reports that figured most closely in the preparation of this book are cited in the reference section. I must pause, however, to take special note of several researcher/writers whose writings were of especial value to me. To that end, I know that I speak for many in the field when I hail the worthy and insightful work of Michael Fullan, Ann Lieberman, Judith Warren Little, and Matthew Miles.

Two other researchers, mentioned earlier in another context, have done work that was of enormous importance to this book in particular: Mary Nordhaus in her documentation of the New Mexico Leadership Academies and John Watkins in his writings on the Trek.

Then, of course, there was the ongoing support of the Rockefeller Foundation. Primarily, this meant having the good fortune to work with Hugh Price, a low-key, open-minded man who is devoted to the proposition that schools can be made better for all children. I appreciate the opportunity that we had for collaboration. I also was helped enormously by two of his colleagues at the foundation with whom I had frequent dealings on this project, Marla Ucelli and Carol Mensah.

Once again, I am pleased to be associated with Teachers College Press in bringing a book to publication. Carole Saltz, the director, and Cathy McClure, my editor, and their various colleagues are consummate professionals who ease a writer's work.

Finally, I thank Ernest Boyer, president of the Carnegie Foundation for the Advancement of Teaching in Princeton, where I have had the privilege to be a senior fellow since 1986. The work I do in contributing to policy reports on education for Carnegie is a helpful complement to my outside writing and keeps me close to a wide variety of educational issues at all levels. I am also indebted to Hinda Greenberg, director of Carnegie's wonderful Information Center (in the old days, it was just called a library), who was helpful in several of my searches.

1

A *climate for team building*

This is the story of an idea for improving schools. The idea is still evolving and the story is incomplete, but enough of it has unfolded both to raise the possibility of team building as a vehicle for school change and to demonstrate how difficult it can be for teams of like-minded people to alter existing practice in their schools. There are lessons here for anyone who works in schools or hopes to work in them, anyone interested in bringing change to schools, and anyone who wonders why schools don't operate more effectively for children.

The tale is told simultaneously on two levels. It is, on one hand, a kind of guidebook for how to go about building a team that might lead the rest of the school community toward improved practice. On the other hand, at the same time, it is an examination of the intricacies of team activities and of the obstacles to teams that inhere in the school structure.

The Leadership Academy—the primary team building effort observed for this book—was the brainchild of the Rockefeller Foundation, a grant-making organization that in recent years has taken a growing interest in the improvement of elementary and secondary schools, especially those that serve America's most disadvantaged children. On the face of it, the approach is simple and straightforward: About a half-dozen teachers, their principal, and perhaps some others associated with the school gather during the summer for several weeks to form themselves into a team that will return to the school in the fall, full of enthusiasm and fresh notions of how to think about making the school better for all children.

An important reason why such a venture is urgently needed is that the much-publicized school reform movement has tended to disregard the role of teachers. It is not that reformers necessarily hold teachers in disdain or even that they are disrespectful of teachers, although such attitudes sometimes undergird strategies for school improvement. More often, it is a case of taking teachers for granted. Proposal after proposal is offered and innovation after innovation is implemented without taking note of the implications for teachers. It is as if designers set out to transform almost every aspect of the automobile without paying attention to the impact on the person who will sit behind the steering wheel.

Such an approach dims the prospects for change. When it comes to schools, teachers cannot be ignored. Recommendations in the name of school improvement must ultimately take account of teachers if education is to be made better. Very little that reaches into the classroom to help students can effectively bypass teachers. If teachers do not endorse an approach, believe in it, and know how to carry it out, then it may be doomed. Consider some of the proposals at the forefront of reform:

- Discipline in schools should be better.
- Achievement levels in math and science should be raised.
- Students should write more in all subjects.
- The school day and/or the school year should be longer.
- There should be more cooperative learning.
- Understanding and problem solving should be emphasized.
- New methods should be used to assess students.
- The drop-out rate should be reduced.
- Systemic change should reach to the core of schooling.

The list could continue ad infinitum. The point is that none of these recommendations can be fully realized without considerable involvement by teachers. The very fact that teachers and teaching have changed so little over the years is indicative of the extent to which schools have continued to operate in the same old ways. Since the 19th century, reform has followed reform and yet schooling appears to be pretty much the same as it always has been (Cuban, 1988). Students have changed far more than teachers have. So if teachers are not integral to the new strategies, there will be no trace of those strategies a few years from now.

Who is going to discipline students? Elves? Just how would math and science instruction improve without teachers being more qualified to provide it? Writing assignments have to be made and marked by someone who can provide informed feedback. What will be done to fill the time if students are to spend more of it productively engaged in school? Students may learn from each other in good cooperative learning, but teachers are needed to organize and oversee this approach, and they can do neither unless they know how. Someone has to teach for understanding. The best assessment is intricately related to instruction, and someone is going to have to do the assessing. Who is going to motivate students who might otherwise become dropouts? How will the heart of the system change without the intense involvement of teachers?

This little lesson in the obvious is intended to overemphasize a point—namely, the folly of imagining there will ever be far-reaching change in schools without linking the efforts to the work of teachers. A fundamental shortcoming of the educational reform movement that has been sweeping across the United States since the early 1980s has been its failure to make the connection between school improvement and teachers. Grandiose plans have scant impact when teachers are unequipped to carry them out.

THE TEACHER'S ROLE

The lack of confidence in the ability of teachers has manifested itself in a rather perverse way. So-called teacher-proof curriculums have been proposed in some locales to overcome the deficiencies of teachers. Those responsible for these curriculums try to bypass the teacher. It is the same kind of attitude as that which Linda Darling-Hammond said typified the educational proposals of the Bush administration—namely, that "teachers don't have enough direction and that they're basically lazy and slothful" (quoted in O'Neil, 1991, p.3). Thus, teacher-proof curriculums arrive in classrooms with orders that teachers are not to deviate one iota from the instructions. In some school systems, this has meant that every elementary school student in the same grade anywhere in the district is expected to be working on the same page of the same textbook as every other student in that grade on a given day. Endorsing this approach is akin to saying that all children born on the same day are supposed to begin to walk, talk, and read on the same days as one another.

The impetus for change, as far as teachers are affected, comes mainly from one of two sources: one external and the other internal to the teacher. Sometimes, the two may overlap.

External change may be triggered by legislation, regulations, or court-enforced directives. Perhaps the most widely recognized example of change induced in this manner has been the racial desegregation of schools by court orders. Troops have even marched onto school grounds to enforce this sort of change. Remedial education is yet another readily recognized example of change that originates external to the teacher, in this case as the result of congressional action. Washington provides almost $7 billion a year to underpin this kind of change by ensuring that remediation is provided by schools. Then there is the unprecedented attention that schools have given to disabled students since 1975, when Congress passed Public Law 94-142, which ordered that the handicapped be educated. Other kinds of changes as well have been pushed onto schools from above. High schools increased the number of years that students had to take math and science to get their diplomas after states adopted new regulations. States and local school districts routinely determine which textbooks teachers are permitted to use. The teacher is in many ways regarded as incidental to such changes.

Change that comes from within the teacher is quite another matter. It may happen in a variety of ways, all of which are of the teacher's own doing. It may occur, for instance, when teachers in an elementary school decide to devote themselves to finding new ways to assess the reading progress of their students and then try to determine the implications for their instructional methods. Or change might be spurred from within if teachers at a high school, for example, decide to immerse themselves in one another's subjects so that they can make the connections that will allow them to show their students the interrelatedness of knowledge or if a group of teachers decides to support one another in developing cooperative learning strategies that will motivate even the least dedicated students. Changes of this sort are internal to teachers in that a kind of personal commitment is needed and the changes are not dictated by exogenous fiat. What is at stake is a knowledge of materials, content, and pedagogy that cannot readily be mandated.

This does not mean that external change should not be attempted because it does not start within the teacher. Sometimes, directives from the outside are the only way to get schools or teachers to modify their behavior in socially or educationally desirable ways. But change that comes from the outside is probably less likely to bring about the kinds of improvements in teaching and learning that students these days require most. Reforms proposed and implemented by those in the building seem to stick better than innovations pushed by outsiders (Tyack, 1991).

Pauly (1991) argues that individual classrooms—not the whole school—account for gains in student achievement. The premise is that ineffective schools are not apt to be turned into effective schools as a result of policies promulgated even at the building level but as a result of what happens classroom by classroom. This is why if an entire school is to change, it must be a cumulative process with the involvement of enough individual teachers. When teams exist, the members can be leaders in fomenting and hastening change in classrooms besides their own. They can be role models and mentors to other teachers in the building. Furthermore, when there is a team, the changes made by individuals can actually be the result of group interaction.

Teachers will certainly have to approach their work differently if schools are to do more to meet the needs of students. There is no way to avoid this conclusion. But, in general, the most practical route to new practice is not by trying to insulate the classroom against the influence of the teacher—as advocates of teacher-proof curriculums would have it—or by trying to dictate change, which has the disadvantage of all top-down directives. Yet, the enthusiasm of policymakers for prescriptive policies that are essentially external to the teacher remains undiminished. They argue that this or that approach would work if only teachers and students would carry out the policies properly (Pauly, 1991).

The point here is not that teachers are perfect but that they are imperfect. And because of their shortcomings, they need help to improve education. No more and no less than those who labor in other pursuits, teachers are wed to the ways of the past. It is abundantly clear that new approaches—carried out by smart, competent teachers—are needed in schools to make learning more substantial and more accessible to students. To the extent that teachers do not take on these roles, schools will fail to change what and how they teach students.

Some teachers can bring about improvement on their own, without help of any sort. These are self-sufficient professionals with a good, intuitive understanding of education who, like an accomplished hockey player streaking toward the cage with a puck, can successfully shift direction without stumbling. But relying on this approach as the way that schools will be made better is like waiting for enough raindrops to fall in order to fill an empty swimming pool. Most teachers, figuratively, cannot skate on their own if the stakes involve substantial change; they require assistance. Restructuring cannot be left to serendipity. It takes planned, focused efforts in which teachers have a key role. Ideally, teachers—once they are convinced and knowledgeable about the changes—will lead and inspire other teachers. Worthwhile change will come when teachers are able to help make it happen. Schools will change when teachers change, individually and collectively.

The Status Quo and Isolation

All too often, the existing organization is not one in which teachers can very readily lead or contribute to change. The organization tends not to bend in response to teachers who pursue change and, in fact, is often is so rigid that it obstructs the possibility of teachers' pushing out in new directions. Many if not most teachers are not equipped to work very differently from the ways in which they now work. Teachers tend to teach the way that they were taught. This is the method that they have seen most, that they know best, and in which they have the most confidence. Furthermore, they seldom have a network of support to sustain them in attempts to try to do it differently. It's fine, for example, to praise cooperative learning or mastery learning, but most teachers will not create settings that foster such innovations in their classrooms until they are persuaded of the merits of the proposals, taught how to implement them, and nurtured through their early efforts.

Traditionally, the message to teachers—communicated both subtly and overtly—has been: Stick with the textbook; remain faithful to the curriculum guide and the lesson plan; lecture in the usual ways; aim to meet the demands of norm-referenced, multiple-choice testing; and carry out the job in an unquestioning manner. Teachers do just that. They learn that ingenuity and creativity are not rewarded and may even be penalized.

Thus, teachers and principals usually find it easier to maintain fealty to familiar practices because of this lack of incentive to do otherwise. Essentially, those who work in schools learn that the system does not want to be disturbed. Many of those associated with education—administrators in particular but teachers as well—feel a stake in preserving what exists. At least everyone knows what is going to happen, even if it doesn't work. Top-down bureaucracies depend on predictability and can be reassuring because of the lack of surprise (Sizer, 1984). The status quo is reinforced, and individual teachers are discouraged from taking steps that might result in new practices. This leaves largely untouched an arrangement by which many students do not fulfill their potential, and schooling is nowhere near as effective as it might be.

In the existing situation, teachers tend to keep to themselves professionally, minding their own business and not trying to alter a structure that seems just too big and too forbidding to confront. Conversation about practice is limited. Collaboration is a word for subversives, and growth on the job is limited to gaining weight with approaching middle age. Seldom does the collective professionalism of teachers who work together in a building influence teaching in that building (Little, 1988).

Professional isolation is a curse familiar to most teachers. The adult in the next classroom is not someone in whom to confide about matters of practice because that is too threatening. No one has the least idea, except through rumors, how anyone else teaches because there are no provisions for observing each other. There seems to be no time to keep up with the professional literature. Joint planning and team teaching are not encouraged. In secondary schools, disciplines are as separate as the planets. Each teacher goes about his or her own work as if the classroom were a school building unto itself.

Teaching is an activity that people almost always do alone. It is a paradoxical pursuit, solitary in that it is carried out by one person and yet communal in that a teacher needs students in order to teach. Teachers grow so accustomed to working on their own that often it is difficult for them to imagine the possibilities of collaboration. Even the professional dealings in the school tend to be a series of one-on-one transactions. A principal speaks to or sends a note to an individual teacher. One teacher asks another a question about a student or about a curriculum topic. Gatherings of the entire faculty for professional purposes are infrequent and often resented as intrusions on teachers' time.

Perhaps the main occasion for teachers to gather regularly with other teachers is lunch, a period of social concerns and complaints that is seldom used for productive professional discussions, as though substantive talk about teaching would be as inappropriate as belching at the table. Almost everything about schools, in other words, is oriented toward going it alone on professional matters.

Teamwork for any purpose is foreign to most teachers. The measure of their success usually rests on how adept they are at working on their own. At a time when schools are replete with talk of cooperative learning—an approach that calls for teachers to teach groups of students to collaborate in their learning—there is not a concomitant move toward collaboration between and among teachers. Not only do they seldom collaborate with partners, but they are expected to be neither leaders nor followers of other teachers. The team building of the Leadership Academy is aimed at counteracting such tendencies. It is not simply a matter of helping teachers to become leaders in their schools but of shaping that leadership so that it flows out of cooperation.

Teachers need encouragement if they are going to work with colleagues to bring about change. The team building described in these pages is oriented toward overcoming the separateness of teachers. Those who attend a Leadership Academy are meant to return to their buildings as part of a cadre eager to engage in educational discussions with each other and available for mutual support. Together they are to launch a crusade. The Holy Grail they seek is better education for the students.

For any teacher, even the most dedicated, to act unilaterally on behalf of schoolwide change is exceedingly difficult. Those who have tried single-handedly to make a difference beyond their own classrooms have found the effort wearying, often frustrating, and ultimately unsuccessful. It is an old story: The teacher goes off to a workshop, returns to the school inspired by what he or she has learned, and tries to transmit this knowledge and enthusiasm to the rest of the faculty. They don't want to hear about it. Personal aspirations for educational improvement become shackled by the potential derision of cynical colleagues. Alone and discouraged, the once-enthused teacher retreats to the sanctuary of his or her own classroom, vowing never again to try to do anything that involves an attempt to work with others in the school.

Altering School Culture

Part of what is at work in team building is an attempt to alter the culture of the school; the ways that teachers go about their work; and the content, manner, and quality of their interaction with each other. Using what he calls an anthropological perspective, Weissglass (1992) says the school culture involves attitudes, beliefs, values, and practices that he maintains are often unquestioned. Garmston (1991) says that school culture is a conscious pattern of values, actions, and artifacts that a new kind of staff development would lead educators to reflect on. Either way, the point is that the culture that usually prevails in an elementary or secondary school is not friendly to change.

This is a culture in which anything different tends to be rejected until the faculty feels a need for it. This doesn't mean that nothing new is attempted unless the faculty is favorably disposed. Almost anyone who has spent time in a school building is familiar with innovations that are halfheartedly adopted and soon abandoned. Teachers can be made to do things, but when they feel that the change is unneeded, the chances of success are dimmed. Thus, Sarason (1982) observes that the New Math came to naught because no one formulated the problem of why it was needed so that teachers would be persuaded to unlearn what they already knew and to learn something else. Instead, what occurred was a forced march to the promised land of New Math, and the results should be a warning to those impatient for rapid improvement in schools (Meier, 1992). Teachers will consider changing practice when the change is seen as moving them closer to a goal that they have embraced (Hawley, 1978). So, if the change is not compatible with existing values and behaviors of faculty members, those values and behaviors must be modified to make them receptive to the change (Louis and others, 1981). The influence of a team could be crucial in this process.

Furthermore, once a felt need arises, teachers are more apt to act on it if they think that someone stands ready to satisfy the need (Zaltman & Duncan, 1977). It is, therefore, not just a matter of getting the faculty to see the wisdom of the change but also reassuring them of the availability of assistance in making the change. In other words, teachers need one another's support and, ideally, the backing of their principals. In schools in which this support is available from members of teams, there is a foundation for gravitating toward change. Palmer (1992) speaks of faculty members adopting a movement mentality that allows them to stop resenting the forces that block change and start discovering each other so that they can form groups for mutual support. His focus is on college faculty, but the observation is equally appropriate for those who teach in elementary and secondary schools.

Education might be improved by a nucleus of teachers in each school prepared to be risk takers inside and outside their own classrooms and ready to advance change throughout the school. Change in schools cannot wait for an infusion of new blood. The staffs of schools turn over slowly, especially in these difficult economic times. The latest indications are that attrition for both new and veteran teachers is much lower than previously thought (RAND Corporation, 1991). So, bringing change to individual schools must depend on teachers who are already in those buildings. The torpor must be dispelled, and teachers most inclined to spearhead change should be helped to succeed in this role.

Sergiovanni (1992) maintains that collegiality itself must come to be understood as a form of professional virtue—something that goes far beyond simple congeniality in the workplace. Team building can be the beginning of collegiality where none existed. Teams can produce a sense of community and of shared commitment that diminishes teacher isolation and uncertainty about effectiveness (Arhar, Johnston, & Markle, 1988). After all, without collegiality, there would seem to be little chance of implementing a schoolwide policy of change. Collegiality, as J. Bennett (1991) sees it, starts with an inclination by teachers to get along and involves a disposition on their part to credit other teachers with a share of power and authority and a willingness to overcome isolation and seek the judgment of other teachers on their own work. Getting teachers to view themselves as interdependent rather than as sole practitioners can set the stage for the work of teams, because teachers are more likely to cooperate when barriers to common action are removed and they feel their problems are shared (Little & Bird, 1984).

The empowerment of teachers, in conjunction with collegiality, can help foster a climate of receptivity and openness. Empowerment gains from getting teachers to regard themselves as colleagues who work together toward common professional objectives. Empowerment can be seen as affecting teachers in three crucial ways, each of which has an impact on the other two (Maeroff, 1988):

1. Boosting status so that teachers are regarded differently by themselves and by others
2. Making teachers more knowledgeable so that they have less need to defer to others
3. Allowing teachers access to decision making

Teachers must have greater status—in the way that they see themselves and in the way that others see them—so that their confidence in being able to do their job increases. They must be more knowledgeable about both content and pedagogy because too many of them simply don't know how to do what they have to do differently. They must have access to the decision-making process so that they will have a greater stake in making the school better.

Empowerment does not mean teachers taking over and principals being pushed out. Rather, it signifies a transformation through which more teachers become confident and knowledgeable practitioners—very possibly as members of teams—who are able to play a part in changing their own teaching and in changing their schools.

AVENUES OF TEACHER RENEWAL

Ultimately, team building has the potential to promote fundamental change in schools, something more basic than just another project. The word *restructuring* has been overused in connection with schools. Those concerned about schools cannot even be certain anymore that they have in mind the same issues when referring to restructuring. Certainly, part of restructuring has to include the professionalism of teachers. Rather than use this book for one more discussion of restructuring, let it be said only that team building will be most successful when it changes teachers' heads, getting them to think new thoughts about the fundamental ways in which schools operate.

It follows that professional development and the role it plays in this regard will have to change as well (David, 1991). Men and women who work in schools must come to recognize that at least some of what they do and some of the ways that schools are organized can be different so that students will be better, more fulfilled learners. The common wisdom that has guided individual educators throughout their careers has to be called into question. For example, is a class best organized for instruction when the teacher stands in front lecturing to students endlessly? What are the most effective ways to motivate students and engage them in their learning? What should students be learning and what grasp of the subject is reasonable to expect of them? What are the best ways for students to demonstrate what they know? What can be done to promote the full education of all children, regardless of their diverse backgrounds? Could secondary education be improved by reorganizing the daily class schedule? These are among the key questions that suggest some of the fundamental issues that deserve the attention of teams.

Which Route to Follow?

Teachers pursuing new approaches might consider three possible routes of travel:

1. Reorientation of one teacher at a time
2. Reorientation of the entire faculty at once
3. Reorientation of a team from within the faculty

There is considerable experience in trying to bring about change through the individual teacher. It is in this manner, enrolling on one's own in courses, that teachers pursue the advanced academic credits that win them raises on the pay scale, as if those courses—whatever the content—necessarily make one a better teacher. Also, there are the many institutes to which a teacher can win a fellowship and go off alone during the summer to join teachers who individually are representatives of other schools. This is often a wonderful intellectual experience for participants. And chances are that the teacher is able to infuse his or her own teaching with fresh ardor and new knowledge.

But the impact that an individual teacher has on the rest of the faculty back at the school, as already noted, is usually negligible. There are no guaranteed allies to help alter the atmosphere in the school. Moreover, the negativism and jealousy of colleagues may end up disheartening the teacher who returned to school hoping to stir the waters of change.

On the other hand, whole-faculty in-service meetings, compulsory and unpleasant, are the customary vehicle for pursuing improvement through the entire faculty. On a few designated days, the teachers are ordered to gather and submit to a round of lectures. Cynicism and resentment fill the room. The potential that this approach might have for bringing about change is blunted by its transitory nature and by the feeling of teachers that they have little stake in the proceedings. Certainly, not all in-service of the traditional kind has failed, but, in general, it has not been a successful route to whole-school reform and to lasting change. "What passes for staff development in our schools is usually very sad," said Sandra Feldman, president of New York City's United Federation of Teachers, the largest teachers' union local in the country, at a national gathering of educators in Washington.

It would be desirable if an entire faculty could operate like a well-oiled, smoothly functioning machine. And this may be possible in a small school, especially an elementary school. Or it might be achieved in a new school, formed from scratch with a hand-selected faculty. When it is possible for the faculty to work as a team of the whole, it might be superfluous to form a smaller team. In most instances, however, the faculty is too large and the seeds of change cannot be sown and cultivated in so vast and unruly a garden.

This leaves the third approach, an idea that has gradually been winning adherents. Several teachers working in tandem, inspired by a powerful esprit de corps, may be able to bring change not only to their own classrooms but also to the school at large. A team, as described in this book, could be a potent weapon in the arsenal of change techniques. At its best, the formation of a team can allow those inclined toward change to seize the moment, banding together to begin a process that may eventually win the support of colleagues. Rather than wait for the educational millenium, those ready for change can begin the quest.

A New Conception of Professional Development

Implicit in the team approach to educational change is a conception of professional development that orients the school toward the continuous intellectual renewal of the faculty. The desired atmosphere is one in which change is no more alien than constantly striving to improve teaching and learning. What if schools were to become places not only where students learn but where teachers learn as well? What if the climate and organization of the school were such that teachers were encouraged to collaborate and to pursue professional growth together? Most everyone readily recognizes and acknowledges that schools ought to be places where young people develop and bloom socially and intellectually. But why should students be the only ones in schools who grow?

A true learning community would be one in which all members, adults included, were constantly expanding themselves. Teachers would take some responsibility for the professional welfare and growth not only of students but also of colleagues (Leithwood, 1990). Senge (1990) envisions what he calls the learning organization, which is what he says all organizations in which people work ought to become as part of the evolution of industrial society. This is no less true of schools and of the people who work in them.

Developing a rich learning environment for teachers as well as for students can be a sine qua non of restructuring. Lieberman and her colleagues say that reform movements have come and gone because they have focused solely on providing new programs and curriculums for students or prescriptions for changes in teacher behavior. They say, however, that "investments in teacher learning are what ultimately feed student learning" (Lieberman, Darling-Hammond, & Zuckerman, 1991, p. 3).

As matters now stand, however, programs of professional development seldom end up with groups of teachers working and reflecting together within their buildings to bring about change through a process in which they are constantly expanding themselves professionally. To do this would be a response to what Sarason (1990) seems to have in mind when, from the vantage point of his experience as a clinical psychologist, he asks why there is nothing in schools comparable to the case conference so that teachers could share, discuss, and criticize "tactics, conceptualization, and goals" (p. 144).

Schools tend not to see themselves this way. The prevailing school culture is one that allows a teacher to settle into a rut and, if he or she chooses, remain mired for an entire career. There is, for example, no expectation of research or publication, as there is for teachers in higher education. No one is terribly surprised when a teacher's knowledge grows stale or when a teacher shows little intellectual curiosity. How strange this is for an occupation in which knowledge and growth are supposedly the foundation stones. It is taken for granted that schoolteachers are not a community of learners, even though learning—by children—is their raison d'être.

What is needed is for teachers to be able to foster circumstances that allow students to reach deeper into their subjects, to make connections between and among subjects, to solve problems, and to think creatively. Doing this will probably require more reflection and cooperation by teachers. Such changes are unlikely to occur on a widespread basis merely by chance. Fresh thinking is required for new approaches. One way to hasten the journey might be for team members to sustain each other as they promote change not only in their classrooms but in the entire building as well.

2

An agenda for team building

A response to the question of what might be done to alter the culture of schools lies in reaching rank-and-file teachers who can assume ownership of new ideas for school improvement that are introduced in their schools, along with strategies for implementation, and who can win supporters in the rest of the school community. A phalanx of true believers, numbering the principal in its midst and supported by the central administration, might lead the way to changes that could make schooling rewarding for all children. This is the team at its best—an ideal that is, admittedly, not readily attainable.

Inside the huge wooden horse that the Greek warriors left outside the walled city of Troy were soldiers who, once the horse had been dragged into the city by the curious Trojans, emerged in the dark of night to open the gates and allow their compatriots to enter. Like the Greek soldiers, teams of teachers can be the advance agents of change in their schools. This form of the Trojan horse, however, is not intended to be devious. The goals of the team should be public, and the participation of others should be invited and encouraged, including a role in selecting the members of the team.

In adopting the team concept, schools can borrow from the experience of business. The two sectors share many reasons for team building. Self-managed teams, on which the members have control over everything from work schedules to hiring and sometimes even firing are proliferating in business as a vehicle for increasing efficiency, effectiveness, and motivation. About one in five employers in the United States has such teams (Lublin, 1992). At Toyota of America, for instance, people work in teams that are given time to talk, brainstorm,

14

refine, and then finally establish targets and means of measuring progress (Schmoker, 1992). Sometimes, corporations use teams to advance total quality management, an approach that calls for carefully examining a specific set of problems and developing a process for solving it.

In some places, business has gone to unprecedented lengths to build team spirit. In connection with a car plant it opened in Hungary, Suzuki Motor Corporation of Japan flew Hungarian workers to Japan for indoctrination (R. Cohen, 1992). Consider these assumptions made by experts who advocate teams for business (Wellins, Byham, & Wilson, 1991):

1. Those closest to the work know best how to perform and improve their jobs.
2. Most employees want to feel that they "own" their jobs and are making meaningful contributions to the effectiveness of their organizations.
3. Teams provide possibilities for empowerment that are not available to individual employees. (p. xvi)

Others who have examined the workplace offer still further assumptions on behalf of teams. Peterson and Hillkirk (1991), who subscribe to the theory of participatory corporate management as posited by W. Edwards Deming, maintain in their proposals for redefining the way Americans work that teams offer the following advantages: a synergism that produces more ideas than would be generated by people working alone, a morale boost because people can more easily find reinforcement, and a bottom-up approach. The idea of the workplace functioning as a learning organization, as sketched out by Senge (1990), includes the existence of teams as learning units within the learning organization. He stresses the need to build teams of employees who can learn together, thereby taking advantage of thought as a collective phenomenon. Dialogue among the members of the team is essential, according to Senge, in order "to go beyond any one individual's understanding . . . [and] gain insights that simply could not be achieved individually" (p. 241).

In a well-founded team approach to school improvement, not only does the team exist, but it is created through a team building process. A team of this kind differs from the usual committee or task force that may outwardly resemble a team but that has seldom undergone formal team building. The members of a typical committee or task force in a school are not bound to each other in ways that members of a fully developed team are, nor are they apt to have the skills and knowledge of the change process that are imparted in formal team building.

A team that participates in this process is supposed to be able to take the lead in involving the rest of the school community in bringing about change. Team members learn the dynamics of group activities, and they try to model the process for others. The team members provide support and sustenance for one another and for those in the school community who join the team's efforts. Driven by a common vision, members of a team strive to carry out their work in visible ways that implicitly invite colleagues to be part of the mission. Properly prepared, teams have the potential to introduce and support the kinds of change needed to bring fundamental improvement to elementary and secondary schools.

In following business and industry into team building, schools can draw on some of the same basic assumptions about what factors contribute to a team's success. Larson and LaFasto (1989) conclude that teams that succeed have eight characteristics in common: "(1) a clear, elevating goal; (2) a results-driven structure; (3) competent members; (4) unified commitment; (5) a collaborative climate; (6) standards of excellence; (7) external support and recognition; (8) principled leadership" (p. 26).

A school team has to be carefully built if its members are going to be reasonably able to take on roles that are new to them. Not that team building is a panacea. The best a team can do for a school is to lead a rigorous struggle to professional fulfillment so that the school community might become all that it is capable of being. Team building is a means to an end, rather than the end. If all goes well, a team might be a vehicle for changing the climate and practice in the school so that student achievement may prosper.

When the Rockefeller Foundation decided to mount a program to aid teachers in introducing change in their schools to help at-risk students, the foundation turned its attention to what could be done to reorient veteran teachers to the special circumstances of poor and minority youngsters. The answer was the Leadership Academy, which is bound by neither time nor place. It is, in effect, a continuing conversation that begins in the school with the whole faculty, continues with a small group during an intensive summer retreat, and resumes back in the school, where the small group attempts once again to engage the entire faculty. If an academy is successful, then the atmosphere of the school in which the team works will be inevitably altered, opening the school to the possibility of constructive change for the benefit of students. A good academy for team building has the following attributes:

- Teams of teachers gather over an extended period, altogether free from routines and from the demands of their regular duties.
- Participation is voluntary, with no one compelled to be a part of a team attending the academy.

- The team includes the principal; if not, there is a very good reason why it doesn't.
- Several schools are involved in the same academy, and each school is represented by a team, with a minimum of three or four teachers from the school on the team.
- The curriculum of the academy ensures that the teams are exposed to cutting-edge ideas that will be at the heart of the change that they seek to pursue.
- The team is equipped with a process for analyzing conditions in the school and for devising strategies for improvement.
- The team thinks about how to involve the rest of the school community in the change process.

THE EVOLUTION OF TEAM BUILDING

Beginning in 1990, Leadership Academies were formed by the colleges of education at the University of New Mexico and Michigan State University. Teams of teachers from schools in each state voluntarily attended these academies—receiving stipends—and returned to their schools to try to carry out their work in new ways that would lead to significant change. A third Leadership Academy was added in 1991, cosponsored by the Southern Educational Foundation and Virginia Commonwealth University to work with the Richmond Public Schools.

The Leadership Academy of the Rockefeller Foundation is the fulcrum for this book's discussion of a model for injecting change into schools through team building. The principles of the Leadership Academy and its outcomes provide a framework for the book. This approach still amounts to a pilot program, however, and it is too early to form final judgments. Yet, the growing interest around the country in team building for school change warrants a book-length examination of the phenomenon even at this incipient stage. Only sporadic attempts have been made until recent years to involve teams of teachers in schoolwork in the ways that the academies seek to promote. An important feature of team building is the bottom-up approach to change, which puts destiny in the hands of teachers. After all, teacher leaders warn that no scheme imposed from on high, regardless of how wonderful, will win the support of teachers (Shanker, 1991).

Rockefeller has no patent on team building for school change. Although the findings, observations, and descriptions offered here draw predominantly on the Rockefeller-sponsored experience, the book is to a great extent a synthesis of what has been occurring in similar enterprises under various sponsors. In fact, the use of the term *academy* on these pages in reference to team building is meant generically from this point on and pertains to workshops, institutes, retreats, and programs of the many sponsors that have supported team building. When an observation is specific to the program of the Rockefeller Foundation, the Leadership Academy will be specified.

In looking beyond the territory charted by Rockefeller, my exploration of team building for school change has extended to such enterprises as the academies of the Trek program of the Coalition of Essential Schools, the Minnesota Educational Effectiveness Program, and Accelerated Schools. The book draws as well on features of team building in programs sponsored by the National Education Association and the American Federation of Teachers. Team building, for instance, was crucial to the restructuring efforts of the 12 schools in the Schools of Tomorrow . . . Today project in New York City run by the Teacher Centers Consortium of the United Federation of Teachers. In fact, the findings of that project, as described in 1991 in *Early Lessons in Restructuring Schools* (Lieberman et al.), are strikingly similar to those reported in this book from the Rockefeller Foundation's Leadership Academies and from other sponsors.

Even the National Science Foundation (NSF), which for many years has done an outstanding job of providing in-service education to individual teachers, has been urged to reconsider its approach in order to work with teams from the same school instead of with individuals (Carnegie Commission on Science, Technology and Government, 1991). The team approach is seen as a way to support pursuit of the improvement objectives of the NSF and to overcome institutional resistance to change.

Also, this book is the beneficiary of what has been learned from the team building aspects of programs carried out under such sponsors as Panasonic Foundation, the Los Angeles Educational Partnership, the California Achievement Council's TEAMS II, and the Edna McConnell Clark Foundation. Thus, the mosaic of team building assembled in these pages uses material gathered from a variety of projects. Although Rockefeller's Leadership Academies provide a centerpiece, I have delved into the programs of additional sponsors to gain a wider perspective for the discussion. This allows a more complete analysis of what is still a new and emerging phenomenon in which little is fixed in place and much remains to be determined.

It is said by education's grizzled veterans that nothing is new—that even what seems to be original has a precedent somewhere in the long and checkered history of school experimentation. And so it is with teams as well. Team teaching, for example, was already the rage in the 1950s. By 1964, in a book to which several Harvard professors contributed, team teaching was said to have assumed the dimensions of a major educational movement (Shaplin & Olds). The authors define *team teaching* as two or more teachers working together for planning, instruction, and evaluation for the same group of students. Teamwork of this sort at the elementary level was identified in a book as early as 1959 (Goodlad & Anderson).

With the passage by Congress of the Education of All Handicapped Children Act in 1975 came the staff support team, a school-based problem-solving group with the aim of providing a vehicle for the discussion of issues related to the needs of individual handicapped children whom the staff was trying to serve (Stokes, 1982). Typically, this multidisciplinary team was envisioned as a panel of consultants in the school to whom a teacher could turn for advice on specific matters involving one of the teacher's disabled students. An underlying assumption in the formation of these teams is echoed in the rationale for today's team building—namely, that teachers who cooperate will have a better chance for success than those who labor in isolation. Staff support teams are not to be confused with the teams mandated by the handicapped law for the purpose of evaluating and placing students and for writing individualized educational plans for each of them. The staff support team was to be an underpinning for the teachers themselves.

Key differences between the kinds of teams discussed in this book and teams that previously existed in schools have to do with the process by which teams are trained and the mission of the teams in the school. The Leadership Academies and the workshops, institutes, and retreats studied here have usually been designed to give the team a special cohesiveness and to equip it to deal not only with specific educational problems but also with the dynamics of the change process itself.

Sometimes, teams of this kind have no purpose other than to introduce the change process to the school. The team is made up of surrogates for the faculty who learn an approach for bringing about change that they then teach to colleagues back at the school. This kind of team building is perhaps most original and most integral to this book. It is not simply that the team is going to return to the school to head the governance unit or even that the team members are going to work as a subject matter team or interdisciplinary team—although this may be the case. The team is honed into an instrument that can deal with the change process.

If there is to be change, a school community has to learn how to look at itself, make judgments, and figure out how to get the educational train running on a new track. Seldom are teachers or even principals equipped to do this without an intervention of some sort. Team building—and all that it represents—is the intervention.

J. Watkins (1992) argues that the usual model of school change assumes that there will be substantive conversation among professional colleagues, an assumption that he says is, under most circumstances, problematic for "political, structural, and epistemological reasons" (p. 1). He says that for such conversations to occur, schools need a change process that provides the methods and information for managing discussions that lead to critical inquiry into essential questions. Watkins, a consultant to the Coalition of Essential Schools, was among those who developed the Trek as a way to give schools a process, structure, focus, and setting for the work of change. Teams return to their schools from the academy portion of the Trek and attempt to transfer into the day-to-day life of their colleagues what they have learned about the process of inquiry as a change strategy.

Successful team building at academies of most sponsors is a careful blend of content and process, ensuring that a team has some substantial ideas with which to work as well as the skills to collaborate and to involve others. The goals and the educational substance of team building vary somewhat from academy to academy. If the aim is to make schools more effective places of teaching and learning, then there are few of the nation's almost 90,000 schools that could not gain from team-led change. Elements of team building for school change have much in common from academy to academy.

EXAMPLES OF ACADEMIES

The nature of the changes that the academy supports shapes the agenda for team building. Among the academies examined more closely in this chapter are the Leadership Academies sponsored by the Rockefeller Foundation and run by Michigan State University and by the University of New Mexico. To enlarge the field of consideration, I describe as well some of the other academies that were reviewed in the writing of this book: the academies of the Trek program of the Coalition of Essential Schools, based at Brown University and run throughout the country; the Minnesota Educational Effectiveness Program, overseen by Minnesota's State Education Department for schools in all parts of the state; and the Accelerated Schools program, based at Stanford University and operated throughout the country.

Much of the educational team building of the last several years has been carried out under the aegis of outside sponsors or with at least the extensive involvement of an agency external to the school district. This approach contrasts sharply with the customary in-service operated by a school system for its own teachers and paid for by district funds. Theoretically, a school district or a consortium of school districts could sponsor academies for teachers from their schools—not unlike the approaches that school systems have taken historically toward in-service or what is now often called professional development. This is probably the model that must evolve if team building is to become widespread and cost-effective. A drawback, however, is the connection of school districts to the flawed in-service of the past. Given this spotty history, teachers tend to respond with more trust and enthusiasm to professional development programs connected to outside sponsors who are seen as untainted (Maeroff, 1988). Thus, team building can benefit from ties to sponsors independent of the school district.

Considered in total, the kinds of models set up by Michigan State University, the University of New Mexico, and other sponsors provide a flexible blueprint for helping schools to create academies for team building. The possibilities for outside support for such academies are extensive. Higher education, business, public education funds, state departments of education, county educational support units, and school district central offices can offer the organizational expertise to sponsor academies, whether or not they provide financial backing. Accelerated Schools, for instance, sets up the program and furnishes the experts but expects the participating school districts to pay for the lodging, food, and transportation of participants. Here, then, are examples of several academies and the programs they have provided.

Michigan State University's Leadership Academy

As the Leadership Academies in Michigan were linked to the effort by Michigan State University to create professional development schools (PDS), an overarching mission was to convey to the teams the understanding, skill, and commitment to explore, develop, and implement the PDS program within their buildings. This was done with a special emphasis on the needs of disadvantaged minority students. The setting for the academy in the summer of 1992 was Mackinac Island, a picturesque and isolated spot at the nexus of the state's upper and lower peninsulas.

The substance of the academy was presented in a series of modules developed mostly by professors from the university in conjunction with participants from the academies of previous years. Case studies were often used as a basis for study and discussion. The modules during the two-week residential session dealt with the following topics (Michigan Academy, 1992):

- *Leadership:* An exploration of the reasons why leadership is needed, what is expected of leaders, and the meaning of collaborative leadership
- *Everybody's children:* Enhancement of understanding of the social/emotional, health, and educational issues that affect children and the role of educators in ensuring equal access to knowledge for all children

- *Teaching and learning:* A focus on getting school faculties to begin a process of studying teaching and actively experimenting with their own practices within the context of the many forces that influence the nature of teaching
- *Schools as communities in communities:* Engagement of participants in a highly interactive examination of behavior, attitudes, and assumptions involved in building school, parent, business, and community relationships
- *Resource allocation, budgets, and reform:* Consideration of issues related to the internal allocation of resources in schools and to changing patterns of authority and responsibility that come with shared decision making and management in schools
- *Organizing of schools for instruction:* An examination of the extent to which implementation of new conceptions of teaching and learning requires changes in school organization

In addition to the six modules, sessions on team effectiveness and facilitation were aimed at getting each group from each school to operate as a team. Participants were introduced to the attributes that characterize an effective team and learned about the styles, needs, and preferences of individual members of teams. Specific skills were taught for team building and for group facilitation.

Woven through the modules were presentations and activities to teach teams about the planning process and experiential learning. Teams explored how they could translate what they were learning at the academy into discussion, planning, and action back at the school. The intent of creating experiences through which the modules were taught to the participants was to provide a model that they could in turn use to engage others in the learning process.

The content of the various modules was presented through lectures, discussions, videotapes, and informal activities in addition to the case studies. There was also time for independent study, personal reflection, and journal writing. A list of background readings was available in conjunction with each module.

University of New Mexico's Leadership Academy

The Leadership Academy of the University of New Mexico in 1991 emphasized the information and skills that teachers must have to meet the needs of at-risk students. This translated into providing participants with a foundation for pursuing these goals in their schools (New Mexico Academy, 1991):

- Intensive development of the team itself
- Sensitivity to cultural diversity

- Awareness of factors that are indicators of at-risk status
- Parents as partners
- Interagency collaboration
- Implementation of appropriate instructional strategies
- Methods of alternative assessment
- Site-based management
- Shared decision making

The teams picked the goals for which they wanted to start developing action plans for their schools. They were not expected to pursue all of the goals at the outset, with the idea being that the priorities of the school would dictate which goals got the most attention. Members of teams were supposed to be able to return to their schools as leaders who could help implement strategies for reaching the selected goals. Thus, the teaching of leadership skills figured prominently in the academy. Participants studied a process they could use to try to bring about change in working with the larger school community.

The academy in 1991 was limited to middle schools—only elementary schools had attended in 1990—and the teams learned about and were guided by *Turning Points* (1989), the report on middle schools issued by the Carnegie Council on Adolescent Development. The document sets out these eight key areas for middle schools to address in order to serve young adolescents:

1. Create small communities for learning.
2. Teach a core academic program.
3. Ensure success for all students.
4. Empower teachers and administrators to make decisions.
5. Staff middle-grade schools with teachers who are expert at teaching young adolescents.
6. Improve academic performance through fostering the health and fitness of young adolescents.
7. Reengage families in the education of young adolescents.
8. Connect schools with communities. (p. 9)

By focusing the specific goals of the New Mexico academy through the prism of *Turning Points,* the teams could more distinctly envision their missions. The day-to-day schedule of the four-week residential academy reflected areas that the schools said in advance that they wanted to see addressed. Sessions ranged in length from an hour to an entire day. The topics covered included situational leadership, block scheduling, the role of special education in the middle school, the teacher as researcher, and James Comer's process for involving parents in schools as members of governance teams. Also, sessions dealt with the special needs of students of African American, Native American, and Hispanic American backgrounds.

The Coalition's Trek

The week-long summer academy is part of a year-long process known as the Trek, which is associated with the Coalition of Essential Schools. It is grounded in research findings that support change in secondary schools. The academy strives to help a school manage its own change process, to provide feedback from peers at other schools, and to assist in the development of specific strategies for change. In trying to improve, schools in the coalition are guided by nine tenets of the organization (Coalition of Essential Schools, n.d.[a]):

1. The school should focus on helping adolescents learn to use their minds well.
2. The school's goals should be simple: That each student master a limited number of essential skills and areas of knowledge.
3. The school's goals should apply to all students. . . .
4. Teaching and learning should be personalized. . . .
5. The governing practical metaphor of the school should be student-as-worker, rather than the more familiar metaphor of teacher-as-deliverer-of-instructional-services.
6. The diploma should be awarded upon a successful final demonstration of mastery for graduation—an "Exhibition."
7. The tone of the school should explicitly and self-consciously stress values of unanxious expectation . . . of trust . . . and of decency . . .
8. The principal and teachers should perceive themselves as generalists first . . . and specialists second. . . .
9. Ultimate administrative and budget targets should include, in addition to total student loads per teacher of 80 or fewer pupils, substantial time for collective planning by teachers, competitive salaries for staff and an ultimate per pupil cost not to exceed that at traditional schools by more than 10%.

In addition to activities devoted specifically to team building, three main activities are practiced at the academy—diagnosing, visioning, and planning/acting/reflecting—as tools that the team is to introduce to the rest of the school community to help achieve understanding and change. In fact, the team itself is regarded as a tool for engaging the whole school. The coalition describes the three activities this way (Coalition of Essential Schools, n.d.[b]):

> Diagnosing is the process of understanding a school in its present state and reassessing [the situation] periodically as the school changes. . . . Visioning is the process that helps move a school forward by creating a shared vision of the kind of place the faculty wants the school to become and by refining that vision periodically. . . . Planning/Acting/Reflecting are the concrete activities which lead to visible changes in a school. (pp. 11, 13, 15)

The Minnesota Educational Effectiveness Program

The Minnesota Educational Effectiveness Program, which began in 1984, is designed to help schools to strive toward implementing the research-based characteristics of school effectiveness. The five-day academy facilitates school improvement; views the school as an integrated system consisting of organization, curriculum, and instruction; encourages involvement of everyone in decision making; facilitates school-based decision making; teaches process skills; and provides a structure for networking.

The innovations are supposed to become part of established practice in the school. The research is organized into 15 characteristics as described in various internal materials of the Minnesota Department of Education:

1. "A common sense of purpose and clearly defined goals"
2. "Building-level leadership which encourages and monitors progress toward purposes and goals"
3. "Collaborative planning and collegial relationships among staff and administration in addressing the purposes and goals of the school"
4. "School-site decision making with autonomy in determining the means by which the purpose and goals are to be met"
5. "District-level support for school-site decision making concerning improvement efforts"
6. "A building-level staff and professional development program directed toward school purposes and goals and closely related to the instructional program of the school"
7. "Family involvement in a child's education and family support of the purposes and goals of the school"
8. "School climate which supports the purposes and goals"
9. "Curriculum organization focused on attaining planned outcomes"
10. "Effective management strategies that communicate the seriousness and purposefulness with which the school takes its task are demonstrated in the classroom and school"
11. "High expectations and positive interpersonal relationships for all students are exhibited and communicated"
12. "Flexible grouping patterns based upon student needs are exhibited in the school and the classroom"
13. "Instruction preparation takes into account student needs, learning styles and available resources"
14. "Effective models of teaching are employed to increase academic learning time and student achievement"
15. "Assessment, monitoring and appropriate feedback is provided"

A team that attends the week-long academy usually selects one or two of the characteristics on which to concentrate, in effect acknowledging that all 15 characteristics or even most of them cannot be implemented at once. The two characteristics to which teams are most often drawn first—school climate and school-site management—tend to be regarded as forerunners of the others. As the end of the academy approaches, the team writes a mission statement relating to its role in the school and then develops an action plan as a guide to involving the rest of the school community in the work of improvement. It is, in other words, a plan for planning. The commitment to change is over the long term.

Accelerated Schools

The week-long academy at which teams are built for the Accelerated Schools program is based on the three guiding principles that the program has enunciated for itself ("Three Central Principles," 1991):

- *Unity of purpose:* Striving by "parents, teachers, students, and administrators toward a common set of goals for the school that will be the focal point of everyone's efforts" (p. 10)
- *School-site decisions and responsibility:* Making "important educational decisions," taking "responsibility for implementing those decisions, and taking responsibility for the outcomes of those decisions" (p. 10)
- *Building on strengths:* "[Utilizing] all of the learning resources that students, parents, school staff, and community bring to the educational endeavor" (p. 11)

Teams are encouraged to learn how to free themselves from the constraints often placed on the education of at-risk students. For the teams and eventually for the entire school this means following new paths and abandoning aspects of the status quo that have led nowhere. Accelerated Schools sums up its philosophy by pointing teams in these directions ("What Are Accelerated Schools?" 1991):

- Having "high expectations for *all* students" instead of "labeling certain children as slow learners" (p. 1)
- Setting "deadlines for making such children academically able" instead of relegating them "to remedial classes without setting goals for improvement" (p. 1)
- Combining "relevant curriculum, powerful and diverse instructional techniques and creative school organization to accelerate the progress of all students" instead of "slowing down the pace of instruction for at-risk students" (p. 1)

- Offering "stimulating instructional programs based on problem-solving and interesting applications" instead of "providing instruction based on 'drill and kill' worksheets" (p. 1)
- Systematically identifying "unique challenges" and searching out solutions instead of reaching for the first apparent solution or simply complying with directives handed down from above without teacher input (p. 11)
- Considering parents of students as integral to solutions instead of treating them "as part of the problem" (p. 11)

The team prepares to lead the effort to change a traditional school into an Accelerated School through a process that calls for taking stock, creating a vision, identifying priority areas for action, and creating governance structures. Step by step, this involves using an inquiry approach that in essence means honing strategies for problem solving. Teams prepare for all this in an academy that offers both affective experiences that lead to bonding and cognitive experiences that lead to an understanding of the philosophy of the Accelerated School.

3

Selecting teams ————————

The most visible and dramatic part of team building is the portion that occurs away from the school, usually during the summer. But that is actually only one of four parts of the process. Ideally, the first part takes place at the school before the team goes to the academy. It happens during the school year leading up to the academy, when the entire school community ought to begin thinking about change, start formulating ideas of what the team might help achieve at the school, and become involved in selecting the team.

The second part of team building is the actual academy, usually during the summer, where members of the team learn to think deeper about the substance of the desired changes and how to implement them. This is when the team bonds into a unit that will try to help the entire school to realize its ambitions. The third part of team building occurs during the crucial school year following the academy. This is when the team tries to transmit to the rest of the faculty what it has learned during the summer. The fourth part comes during the succeeding years, when involvement in change will grow and the team will either make a breakthrough or find that it cannot spread its influence very far into the school community.

Team building begins, in effect, before there is a team and even before the schools that are going to be asked to choose teams are identified. In most school systems of substantial size, there is unlikely to be enough money at the outset to enable every school to be part of an academy. Thus, the first step is to identify schools that will participate.

CHOOSING A SCHOOL

Selecting schools for an academy often entails asking the superintendent to recommend the schools in the district that would be good candidates. Two purposes are served by such a request. Presumably, the superintendent—relying on the advice of top aides—has a good overview of the district and knows which schools are apt to gain most from team building. Equally important, initiating the process through the superintendent heightens the chances of winning the allegiance of central authorities at the outset. But this approach is not foolproof. One sponsor found that a superintendent who was asked to recommend schools for an academy either had poor judgment or harbored a political agenda. The schools represented at the academy at his suggestion turned out to be poor choices.

Another approach is to work directly through the schools in searching for those that will send teams to an academy. The mail and personal contact can be used to solicit inquiries and applications. The district office will probably be kept informed of the process, but it may be mainly up to the principal and the school community to decide if the school wants to apply to participate. Because the support of the district office will ultimately be so important to the team and to the school, it is desirable that the sponsor cultivate good relations with headquarters officials even if they are not designating the schools.

Almost all sponsors try to elicit commitments from the schools as a quid pro quo for attending an academy. Both the Coalition of Essential Schools and Accelerated Schools ask that at least 75% of the faculty commit themselves in advance to the concepts represented by their academies. To be eligible to attend an academy sponsored by Accelerated Schools, for instance, a school must submit a letter signed by at least three quarters of the full-time teachers who work in the building. "We really want to encourage school staffs to explore the idea of the Accelerated School before deciding to attend the summer academy," the application proclaims to those who are interested. "We have learned painfully through experience that those staffs that have been 'anointed' by an administrator to become Accelerated Schools often fail to successfully implement the concepts."

As a further mark of commitment, Accelerated Schools asks the school to send, along with the application, a check covering housing and food costs for the school team. The amount is refundable if the school is not chosen. "This shows that the school has the wherewithal to cut through the bureaucracy and get the money," said Brenda LeTendre, training coordinator for Accelerated Schools. Presumably, it is this same ability to pierce the bureaucracy that will be needed to bring change to the school.

Schools That Benefit Most from an Academy

One debate about team building has to do with whether the prime candidates should be the schools with the greatest likelihood of success or the schools most desperately in need of change. It is a matter of setting priorities for the use of scarce resources, a kind of educational triage. It seems reasonable to concentrate on schools where team building is most likely to pay dividends.

Yet, some advocates of team building maintain that the schools that are ailing most should get preference because that is where the process is most needed. The California Achievement Council, in its TEAMS II team building program, for example, deliberately seeks schools with poor teacher morale, high teacher turnover, and low student achievement. Its participating schools are all situated in poor neighborhoods. The acronym TEAMS stands for Teaching Excellence for Achievement in Minority Schools.

There is no disputing that troubled schools could benefit most from change. But the very conditions that put such a school in dire straits may well undermine a team's prospects. It is important, for instance, that a principal be receptive to the idea of team building and that there be at least a critical core of teachers who are dedicated to uprooting the status quo. In the absence of these prerequisites, trying to introduce change through the team approach is chancy. Relationships among staff members at such schools may be so dysfunctional that the staff members do not appear ready to build a cohesive team or to provide a supportive environment in which the team can operate when it returns to the school. Sometimes, however, teams from such schools turn out to thrive at an academy and have a surprisingly favorable impact on their schools.

At one academy, for instance, such a school was represented by a team on which a member, the assistant principal, was suing another member, a department chair. Meanwhile, the department chair had a grievance pending against that same assistant principal. Most of the building's teachers, including those at the academy, sided with the department chair in the dispute. The air around the table was charged with tension as the six individuals who were supposed to be forming themselves into a team sat together during the first days of the academy. There seemed to be a real question of whether the school should have been invited to send a team under the circumstances. The need for change, however, was indisputable. This was a middle school in an impoverished town where low academic achievement was the rule.

What triggered the disagreement was a survey requested by the principal, who sought to discover why dissatisfaction was rife among the faculty. The principal had asked each chair to talk with the department's teachers and report to him on the causes of the unrest. The department chair who ended up on the team had responded with a memo saying that the teachers found the assistant principal unsupportive. The assistant principal saw the memo and asked the department chair to withdraw it. She refused, and turmoil erupted. It wasn't until two days before the academy was to begin that the sponsor learned of the conflict within the team.

The story is complicated by the progress that the team eventually made at the academy and during the ensuing school year. After getting to know each other better, the two feuding members agreed to call off the litigation and the grievance. Furthermore, one of the members of the team was elevated after the summer to join the school administration as an assistant principal, replacing the previous assistant principal, who left the team. Also, the principal, who joined the team for the last half of the academy, became a productive member. This team truly led its school toward confronting some of its problems. It is doubtful, according to the sponsor of the academy, that there would have been such a turn of events without benefit of the school's participation in the academy.

Mixing Different Kinds of Schools

Setting criteria for schools that are to attend an academy also means thinking about the extent to which elementary schools, middle schools, and high schools ought to be mixed during the team building process. Some academies are restricted to schools at one level, and others cut across the levels. There is even a question of whether team building can be as effective at the secondary level as at the elementary level. The organization of the faculty is structurally different from one level to the other, perhaps dictating different approaches to team building. One review of various projects found that the higher the grade level, the more resistant to training was the teacher. High school teachers were more insulated and independent and were more apt to blame students for the failure of the schools (Mann, 1987).

It is probably more difficult to meet the diverse needs of teams that attend the same academy if they are not all from schools of the same grade levels. Mixing schools of different levels, however, offers the advantage of perhaps a richer experience for the participants, particularly when the schools are part of a feeder pattern. There is, after all, a potential for problems if a school at one level—say, the middle school—makes substantial changes in its structure, content, and pedagogy and educates students in a setting philosophically unlike that which they will encounter in high school. When schools from different grade levels attend the same academy, it is not uncommon for some sessions to be organized by grade levels. The TEAMS II program of the Achievement Council always assembles teams from schools on all three levels and then has breakout sessions by grade level at different points during the academy.

There is yet another consideration in regard to how much the schools should have in common. Even at the same level, schools tend not to have equal amounts of sophistication. For example, in connection with the Leadership Academy sponsored by the University of New Mexico in 1990, Nordhaus (1990) notes:

> . . . some school teams come from faculties where the change process is under way, other school teams (one from a new school still under construction) were composed of people who had not worked together before. Some teams arrived at the academy armed with needs assessments for their sites and directives from school committees. Others arrived empty handed, and began work from scratch. (p. 3)

Teachers who have prior knowledge of the kind of information and skills presented at an academy or teams that have already been working together and have incorporated group process skills into their approach may be poorly served by an academy that starts all teams at the beginning. On the other hand, the challenge facing an academy that accommodates teams of diverse sophistication might be seen as analogous to that which teachers encounter when they try to replace homogeneous grouping with heterogeneous grouping.

The size of the team is yet another factor that has an impact both on team building and on the team's ability to carry out its work in the school. A team with too few members is one in which each member may end up with too much to do and too small a network of support. But having too many on a team can impede the team building process by limiting the level of intimacy and bonding that is possible. As a rule of thumb, a team should have at least three or four members. After observation and study of academies under various sponsors, it appears that four to eight is probably the most frequently desired size for a team in a school. It is possible to build a team with 10 to 15 members, although this is verging on too many. One point to consider is that the more members on the team, the more apt they are to break into cliques. Such divisiveness can be inimical to team building. A survey of teams in industry found that the average size was 6 to 12 members (Wellins et al., 1991).

A consideration in fixing the size of the team is the size of the school. Six people represent 25% of a faculty of 24, but they are only 10% of a faculty of 60. Teams of a half-dozen members will usually suffice for elementary schools, but a slightly larger team may be needed for a typical secondary school because the faculty is bigger. There is a dilemma, however, as far as secondary schools are concerned. Too small a team may be inadequate for representing the constituencies and for taking on the work of improvement throughout the school, but too large a group may never really congeal as a team.

What becomes apparent in observing educators together in the setting of an academy is that the dynamics that create a team from out of a group of individuals cannot readily be put in place in a day or two, which historically has been the length of a faculty retreat—for the few teachers lucky enough to attend a retreat. Team building takes time— probably at least a week and possibly two or three weeks—if the money and time are available. There is virtue in simply putting people in proximity and then letting them stay at close quarters for a while to work out problems that are presented to them, compelling them to use group process procedures in a kind of experiential learning. It is like marinating food that is to be grilled; it must remain in the marinade long enough to take on the desired flavor. A team is not a team until the members are able to work together smoothly and efficiently.

The School Gets Ready

Once a school is identified for team building, the entire school community should come to understand what will be at stake. It will be counterproductive if a team is chosen and the rest of the faculty regard an academy as something to which they are unconnected. Everyone at the school should be impressed with the idea that the team members are their surrogates and that the team is not to be regarded as a separate entity that will operate external to the rest of the school. In other words, ownership should be spread and shared from the outset. Teams sometimes fail because they are perceived by the rest of the school community as apart from everyone else and as pursuing an agenda of their own that has little do with the rest of the school. Steps must be taken even before team building starts so as to avoid this stigma. Part of the legitimacy of the group that will manage change in the school is conferred "at the front end," so it is understood in advance what kinds of decisions the group is going to be able to make and what money it will be able to spend (Fullan & Miles, 1992, p. 751).

That is why it is a good idea to precede the academy with a period during which the school community assesses its situation and considers the possibilities for change. The school year leading up to the summer academy can be a time for introspection. What happens during this period might be likened to what occurs as a school or college prepares for a visit by the representatives of a regional accrediting association. In such instances, there is usually an institutional self-study. A school that better understands itself can gain the most from team building and will be most receptive to the overtures of the returning team.

There is an inherent contradiction here, however, that must be acknowledged. If the school were fully able to carry out such a self-analysis, recognizing the implications of the findings and proposing appropriate adjustments, then the team building and the academy might be superfluous. The fact that as matters now stand, so many schools are incapable of professional reflection and unequipped to deal with the consequences is a reason why team building is needed.

Thus, it is desirable for the school community go through these various steps in the months leading up to the academy, but it is because of the school's limited capacity for reflection, analysis, and action that the academy is needed. The upshot is that the raising of consciousness that takes place in the school prior to the academy and prior to the team's existence may be truncated. Nonetheless, doing whatever is possible to put the school under a microscope may offer at least these advantages:

- It signals that what is about to happen is intended to have relevance to everyone in the school, not just to the team.
- It lets the school community start focusing on conditions in the school and on what might happen to move improvement forward.
- It offers people the chance to think about themselves as potential members of the team and to weigh their own commitment.
- It permits wider input into the decisions about who will be on the team.
- It gives those who end up on the team some advance knowledge of the changes that would be most valued by the entire faculty.

THE TEAM'S RELATIONSHIP TO THE SCHOOL

The role that a team is to play in a school helps to determine the composition of the team. There are any number of ways that a team built in an academy might carry out its work in the school, and some people who are suitable members of one kind of team might not appropriately serve on a different sort of team. As spelled out in chapter 2, the kind of team building with which this book is mainly concerned is the sort that produces a group that learns the dynamics of the change process and then returns to the school to share the approach with the larger community. What is called *systemic change,* as the phrase implies, will ultimately touch every phase of the school and everyone associated with the school.

Some advocates of systemic change maintain that it is fruitless to strive for anything less. They say that a school cannot be changed piece by piece. Yet, there are many schools that for one reason or another seek something less than systemic change. The purpose of team building in these instances may be to concentrate on one part of the school or on one aspect of the school's operations. These, too, can be legitimate aims of team building.

Perhaps the most prevalent reason for team building is to prepare for school-based management. A group from the school community is equipped to take on governance responsibilities. In fact, some people assume that this is the main—if not the sole—reason for team building. But there are other ways as well in which teams might function in trying to promote change. Teams might be set up along the following lines:

> Governance teams
> Subject matter teams
> Grade-level teams
> Pedagogy teams
> Interdisciplinary teams
> Multipurpose teams

Governance Teams

The adoption of school-based management and of shared decision making implies that a group from the school be ready and willing to take some responsibility for the destiny of the school. State mandates in such places as Texas and California have prodded this move and have led to the creation of governance teams in schools that had never before considered creating such bodies. Similarly, in such local school districts as Dade County, Florida, and New York City, teams have been formed in many schools to share the decision making for school-based management. Team building for any number of specific pedagogical purposes can piggyback on these governance teams. In Texas, for instance, members of the mandated school councils became members of the teams that attended the academies sponsored by Accelerated Schools.

Often, however, there is no mention of how governance teams are miraculously supposed to know how to handle the new duties. It is as if the tooth fairy will appear with a magic wand and consecrate the team so it can assume a role for which it has received no preparation. Merely delegating authority for school-based management does not automatically release teachers' expertise (Mutchler & Duttweiler, n.d.).

Thus, team building can be a step toward filling this gap by helping those in the governance group to learn group processing skills that will enable them, say, to deal with conflict. As a result of undergoing formal team building, teams are also more likely to reach the point at which they subscribe to a common vision that guides and informs their work. Team building for the purpose of governance might be done even at schools that are not officially operating under school-based management. It may be that the contribution of the team members to governance comes from participating on school committees.

At one school, for instance, each member of the team that had been built at an academy assumed a leadership role on one of the several task forces that were set up to deal with various aspects of the school's operation: transportation, lunch, parent relations, and playground. These task forces were obviously not at the apex of pedagogical concerns, but members of the team nonetheless became important leaders in what that particular school was ready to let teachers do outside the classroom.

Subject Matter Teams

Team building has a special appeal to high school teachers when it is done in conjunction with the disciplines they teach. Organizing a team around subject matter quickly gets teachers to the heart of their work. This is a way to overcome isolation and to encourage colleagueship. Members of a subject matter team will probably not work together in the same classroom, but as a result of being on a team, they will be more inclined to talk regularly with one another about aspects of the content and pedagogy of their subject.

In attempting to spur change in mathematics, the Los Angeles Educational Partnership (LAEP) worked with the entire math departments of several high schools in a program known as +Plus+. The department in effect became the team. The program called for each math department to set a succinct goal for improving student learning. The department developed a strategy for reaching the goal, enumerated the steps toward the goal, and determined the evidence that could be viewed as a sign of success. The team formulated a timetable, a budget, and a plan for using released time and professional consultation. Each department/team got a $2,500 grant from LAEP to carry out its work and an additional $500 to hire a consultant. On top of this, incentive awards of $250 each were paid to the teams to implement distinguishing features of their improvement plans.

To link the schools, each math department/team chose a lead person to attend the +Plus+ meetings of the participating schools. This was a forum in which ideas and strategies of the various departments could be exchanged and additional needs could be identified.

Subject matter teams need not be limited to secondary schools. Many benefits can flow to elementary-level teachers who are bound by interest in a subject. As all elementary school teachers are responsible for mathematics instruction, as they are for all the other main subjects, a mathematics team in the school could, for example, include volunteers from various grade levels. Such a team might help teachers to strengthen their ability to teach a subject in which so many of them are weak and lacking in confidence. As matters now stand, the math courses that future elementary school teachers take in college neither contain a serious treatment of the arithmetic and geometric ideas central to elementary mathematics nor are taught in ways that model effective teaching (Cipra, 1992).

Grade-Level Teams

Teachers, especially in elementary and middle schools, can very naturally organize themselves around grade levels. Such an approach could be seen in Wells Junior High School—a middle school in all but name—in southern Maine, where grade-level teams were formed at the sixth, seventh, and eighth grades. Each team consisted of a teacher for math, social studies, science, language arts, and reading. A group of 110 students was assigned to each five-member grade-level team.

Every day, the team got 80 minutes without students, who during that time attended classes for computer literacy, art, or band. The team decided how to apportion its time without the students so as to spend part of it working together and part of it working individually. One member of each of the three grade-level teams was selected as leader and received a stipend to represent the team on the building leadership team, which concerned itself with governance decisions on a school-wide basis.

Pedagogy Teams

Team building that stems from a shared interest in pedagogy can bring together faculty members across the disciplines or across grade levels. The term *pedagogy* is used loosely here, but the point is that a team in an elementary school or a secondary school might be organized around a professional interest having to do with teaching and learning as, for example, cooperative education, technology, or alternative assessment. Such a team can be the locus for gaining new knowledge, celebrating successes, examining failures, and creating a culture that will spread beyond the team. Sometimes, a team of this sort is known as a study group.

Kendon School in Lansing, Michigan, formed home literacy teams to promote the literacy growth of students through ties that the teachers would make to parents. The teams worked under the guidance of a Michigan State University professor who sought to help each team to tailor its efforts specifically to its grade level. A goal was to increase the capability, responsibility, and willingness of parents to support the literacy development of their children. The professor used her participation as an opportunity to conduct research on parent involvement.

The two members of the kindergarten team decided that they were not meeting the main literacy objectives they had set for the students: increased self-esteem for the children, growth in language, and better listening skills. A teaching device that they took for granted—show-and-tell—became the medium for this team's efforts to build literacy and to involve parents. The teachers interviewed kindergarten teachers elsewhere in the district to find out how and to what effect they used show-and-tell. Notes were sent to parents every Friday asking that they help their children to prepare presentations for show-and-tell. Sometimes, this might involve sending home yarn and construction paper with the children and asking parents to make valentines with them so that the children could show the valentines and tell how they were made. Some parents were invited to the school and were coached on how to assist their children at home.

The first-grade team sought to bolster parents' understanding of their children's development as readers and as writers. "Parents weren't respecting this growth in their children," said a teacher. "They didn't appreciate the work that the children were doing in becoming more literate. We would send things home and ask the parents to work with the children, and they weren't communicating." The first-grade home literacy team held four parent forums at four different times of the day to give parents fewer excuses for not attending.

The professor helped make the home literacy teams into vehicles for the growth of teachers as well as of students and parents. The teachers joined her in making presentations on their work at scholarly meetings at which she presented papers on her findings.

Interdisciplinary Teams

A national model for interdisciplinary team building has been the Humanitas project sponsored by LAEP. Each team has at least three and often four members, usually drawn from social studies, English, and art. The team develops core units organized around five or six conceptual themes, cutting across the disciplines, which can be taught collaboratively at one grade level in a school-within-a-school-type setting. If the team building occurs during the summer, the academy lasts for two weeks, and if it is done during the school year, the team is released for a one-week academy. Once a team goes through an academy and is offering its interdisciplinary program to students, team members may return for further work at academies in succeeding summers.

An example of a six-week unit developed through Humanitas was "A Twentieth Century Dilemma: Me or We?" for ninth graders at a high school in Los Angeles. The social studies teacher taught about social institutions by exploring such topics as urbanization, alienation, suburbanization, and race issues, using readings from such writers as Vance Packard and Max Weber. The English teacher developed such topics as assimilation, ostracism, socialization, the need to belong, and the need for individuality. She drew on such works as Salinger's *Catcher in the Rye,* the Harlem Renaissance poets, and the film *West Side Story.* The art teacher dealt with Ruscha, Rauschenburg, Quakertown architecture, city planning, graffiti art, and self-portraits that the students were to make in the form of collages. Also, she included study of the blues, punk rock, rap, and the work of the Beatles.

The members of a Humanitas team are supposed to share a daily preparation period once they return to the school to implement their program, but this was not always followed. An evaluator found that the least successful Humanitas teams were those on which there was insufficient ongoing collaboration, which led individuals to try to carry out an interdisciplinary program without meeting frequently enough to share feedback and revise plans (Aschbacher, 1991).

Multipurpose Teams

The role of a team may overlap among two or more of the various purposes described here. For example, a grade-level team might also organize itself around the exploration of a particular pedagogy. Or a governance team might be made up of a group of teachers working together on an interdisciplinary program, especially in a school-within-a-school arrangement. The point is that the purpose of team building is not always structured so that members of teams end up performing along only one dimension.

It might be possible, for instance, for a pedagogy team that is trying to figure out how to change the grouping in a school so as to end tracking to evolve into another sort of team. In moving from homogeneous grouping to heterogeneous grouping, the comprehensive changes required of the teachers might cause them to alter significantly the ways in which they work together (Oakes & Lipton, 1992). The teachers could conceivably form grade-level teams or subject matter teams to pool their resources so that new lessons could be prepared for the new approach. Or they might work as an interdisciplinary team toward the goal of untracking the curriculum.

SELECTING INDIVIDUALS

A discovery made in retrospect by some early academies is that when teams are selected too close to the end of the school year, not enough time is available for the first phase—the period before the academy—when the whole school community is supposed to be involved. There is insufficient time to consider who should be on the team; nor, once chosen, do members of the team have enough time to think about and plan for the adventure on which they are about to embark.

Whether or not teams are chosen too early, they sometimes end up including some members who probably should not have been selected: people about to retire or on the verge of transferring out of the school. Such people are in no position to advance improvement in the schools they represent at the academy. Clearly, schools should resist putting certain members on teams. This may mean omitting not only those whose relationship with the school is about to be severed but also members of the school community whose only qualification is that they are available to attend the academy.

In other words, teams should not be formed by default. This is a bigger problem than might be immediately apparent. More than 70% of elementary and secondary teachers are women, and many are mothers with primary responsibility for child care, especially during the summer when children are home on vacation. Society may be sexist in this regard, but this is the reality of the situation. Schools often find that those who ought to be prime candidates for team building cannot attend academies because they are not able to be away from home for an extended period during the summer. Unfortunately, this sometimes means sending participants who are less than ideal candidates for team building, drafting members for teams simply because they have no small children to mind, or—as I found in some instances—including some people on teams merely because they were the ones whose spouses would allow them to go.

Sponsors of academies find it productive to visit a school after it has been selected but before the team has been chosen so as to discuss the composition of the team and what the academy hopes to accomplish for the team, the school, and, most important, for the students who attend the school. One sponsor encourages schools to measure potential participants by six criteria:

- Commitment to change
- A reputation for innovation
- An ability to make things happen
- Evidence of energy and persistence

- Evidence of some capacity for leadership based on past performance or the perception of others
- Patience

Sometimes, membership on the team is automatically conferred—for example, if a governance group already exists in the school and the aim is to give that group more coherence as a team. The academy and the team building process may offer a chance for the group to gain cohesion and skills that will allow it to thrive as a decision-making body. This is an entirely reasonable basis for designating the members of a team. Alternatively, a team may automatically include all the teachers at a particular grade level if the goal is to build teams at that grade.

No One Best Way

There seem to be as many ways to select members of teams as there are schools sending teams. So far in the various experiences with team building, no one method of team selection has emerged as best or guaranteed to produce the finest team. Teams for the Rockefeller Foundation's Leadership Academies were formed in various ways, ranging from teams that were simply named by the principal to those that were made up of volunteers who happened to be the only ones in the building who wanted to attend. Some teams were elected in straight popularity contests that neither ensured balance on the team nor guaranteed that various constituencies in the school were represented on the team. The following are some of the ways that schools in general select the members of teams:

- Volunteers sign up until enough have enlisted to form a team.
- An election is held, and those who get the most votes are put on the team.
- The principal designates the team members.
- Members of an existing group, such as a faculty advisory council or a group of teachers trying to develop an interdisciplinary curriculum, become the team.
- Any combination of the above.

Usually, it is preferable that members of a team serve out of conviction—not simply because they were asked, ordered, or elected to membership. A lack of enthusiasm sours the milieu for team building. Change in schools should begin, at least in part, with those most inclined toward and most sympathetic to breaking with the status quo.

On the other hand, although the idea of leaning toward volunteers is appealing, researchers assert that "the widespread assumption that voluntarism increases both motivation and the likelihood to use the content of training has not been tested by its chief advocates" (Joyce, Bennett, & Rolheiser-Bennett, 1990, p. 35).

Having on the team those who are seemingly most favorable to change, in other words, may not ensure success. The Panasonic Foundation has been supporting school improvement since 1987, establishing partnerships that are to last between 5 and 10 years with nine urban school districts. The foundation had a policy at one point of trying to cultivate the involvement of those who seemed most committed to change. An evaluator noted, however, that there were drawbacks to the "empower the movers" strategy, which sometimes empowered rebels who had a commitment to change "but were not the right people to bring others along" (Mitchell, 1990, p. 9).

It is, of course, desirable to assemble a team in which the members have potential for working together and for becoming leaders in the school. Balance among the various grades is helpful at the elementary level, and balance among subject areas is equally important at the secondary level. The Coalition of Essential Schools suggests that a school that is going to participate in the Trek academy include on its team at least four people who represent different levels or functions within the school or district. Representation of various factions in the school ought to be considered as well.

De facto lines of communication must also be recognized, as informal as they may be. Schools that select participants for the Minnesota Educational Effectiveness Program are encouraged to try to get factions in the faculty represented on the team. Team members are asked to think of themselves not only as emissaries *from* the factions but as emissaries *to* the factions. This is seen as a way of promoting communication by the team with the rest of the faculty. Ultimately, members of a team have to be able to get the attention of the rest of the school community.

A middle school principal on a team that attended one of the academies had personally appointed the team and put himself on it, but only after going through a process that he thought would produce a group with strong potential for changing the school. Thus, he asked each teacher in the school to submit a list of the names of colleagues in the school whom each considered to have the greatest credibility. At the same time, the principal asked those who wanted to volunteer for the academy to submit their own names. Then he chose the team by matching the list of volunteers with the list of those whom peers deemed most credible. Whatever manner is used to select the team, the following guidelines can help:

- The choice of who is on the team probably should not be imposed, which means that even a principal who names a team should consult with others.
- Efforts should be made to include some of those in the building who are already leaders or who have the greatest promise of becoming leaders.
- The diversity of the faculty and the student body should be considered.
- Precious space should not be wasted on someone who is not apt to remain in the building for several more years.
- Attention should be given to the informal faculty cliques that exist in the school and to how they will react to the team's composition.
- Natural divisions in the school—grade levels in an elementary school and subject areas in a secondary school—should be considered.
- The pivotal position of the teachers' collective bargaining unit should be recognized so that the union is at least a party to the discussions.

Selecting Those Other Than Teachers

A main decision with regard to the team's composition has to do with the extent to which members other than teachers and the principal should be included. Schools usually feel comfortable sending a guidance counselor, a librarian, or a reading specialist as part of the contingent. Educational aides also serve as members of some teams. As a matter of fact, educational aides sometimes turn out to be surprisingly influential in the school community after the academy. This was so in the case of one aide, who got such a boost from her experience at the academy and from her membership on the team that the teacher to whose classroom she was assigned was jealous of her elevated status. The aide had to be reassigned to another teacher.

Picking members of teams is particularly complex when it comes to those who are not actually employed in the school. Decisions on these members may be driven more by political considerations than by educational ones. The three main groups that figure in this regard are the central administration, the school board, and the parents. Infrequently, students may serve on teams.

A central administrator as a team member can be in a position to help unscramble bureaucratic procedures that so often thwart efforts to bring about change. In fact, Accelerated Schools requires that each team include a "central office advocate," and some other sponsors recommend that someone in a ranking position in the central office be named to the team. Having such a person on a team is apt to enhance continuity because the administrator is not someone who is going to transfer to another building, as might happen with a teacher or a principal on the team. But an administrator from the central office has his or her own job to do and can render only limited service to the school community. So, putting a central office administrator on the team could well mean having one person fewer who is in the building every day on a full-time basis to help the team.

A school board member on a team could be a guardian on high for the school, protecting the building from the vicissitudes of fickle central administrators. But such a person, as a nonemployee, is not likely to have the natural affinity with other members of the team—and with the rest of the faculty—that someone who works in the school or at least for the district is apt to have. Furthermore, like a central administrator, a school board member is not likely to be around to aid and sustain the rest of the team on a full-time basis.

Most problematic of all is the parent as a team member. The case for including parents on teams is obvious. Parents are the ones whose offspring are to be the recipients of whatever benefits team building confers on a school. Therefore, parents have a huge stake in team building for school improvement. Districts across the country often have a mandate to include parents in the governance structure when implementing school-based management. Furthermore, having a parent as a teammate gives the professionals on the team a perspective they may otherwise lack as well as easier access to other parents of students.

Such arguments seem incontrovertible. Yet, there are some reasons why it might not be desirable to have parents on teams that are built at academies. Parents do not work in the school, and although they have a stake in the school, it is a stake of a different kind. Parents are not professional educators. This does not mean that they should not be heard or that they should not be heeded. But team building through an academy tends to be about much more than simply forming a governance unit. These are people who will labor elbow to elbow each day as colleagues in the pursuit they have chosen as their life's work. Team building is about bonding and enhancing such people as professionals.

Parents need not take umbrage if they are not included in team building of this sort. This does not mean, however, that team building should give license to ignore parents or even to try to diminish their influence on the school. It ought to be obvious by now that the speediest route to higher academic achievement by students is through the home. Ways must be developed to align school and home so that what happens out of school reinforces the educational mission. This is immeasurably easier when parents feel at one with the school. And finally, if after weighing these various arguments it is decided to include parents on the team, this should mean *full* participation. The parent should go through the academy with the team and should be an equal partner in the team's work in the school, although some of the parent's responsibilities may differ—as they inevitably will for each member of the team.

The Special Case of the Union

The union chapter in the school must be taken into consideration in team building. To do otherwise is to court failure. The union, especially when collective bargaining exists, is most often the voice of the teachers. Like the principal or the superintendent, the union leadership can do much to block the success of team building if it so chooses.

Early in the process—probably before the school is even selected—the union should be reassured about team building—that it is a vehicle for neither undermining the union nor finding a detour around contractual agreements. The union must, however, recognize that a team has to have a measure of autonomy and that team members should be able to give of their own time without recompense under some circumstances. Teams are about professionalism, and if members must be compensated for every act they perform, then team building is apt to be doomed. In some places, the union decides to take an active role in selecting the team and remains involved in the team's work. Elsewhere, the union is satisfied to be a passive partner to team building.

Where the union's connection to team building becomes most complicated is a school in which the union has been a part of the school's problem. Just as there are some unenlightened principals, there are some equally unenlightened local union officers. Team building is questionable when it appears that an unreasonable and intransigent union local would be an albatross around the neck of the team. On the other hand, serious conversations about whether to attempt to build a team might be the beginning of a new era in a school in which not enough has been done to win the partnership of the union in school improvement.

A TEAM'S CONCERNS ABOUT CHANGE

The journey of change may be an endless trip in which, like a mirage, the destination recedes each time it appears near. What a team faces upon embarking on such an expedition was illustrated at the start of an academy in Michigan by one of the teams as it took time to address the meaning of change for the team and for the school at large. The areas in which members of the team challenged themselves have relevance to all teams that enter team building. The team struggled to come to terms with answers to the following five questions:

1. Why are we changing?
2. What are we worried about losing or leaving behind?
3. What are we most uncertain about?
4. What do we have to unlearn?
5. What are we committing ourselves to?

As the team from this elementary school pondered the first question—why the school had decided to make changes—they determined that change was necessary mostly because what was being done at the school was not working well enough and because the circumstances in which the school operated had changed, even if the manner in which they taught had not. The team acknowledged that there were contradictions between the ways in which they thought the children should be educated and the ways in which students in the school were actually being educated. The team believed the school was not meeting the needs of the students.

In part, the team concluded, this was because the larger society in which the school operated and the support structures that underpinned the children were changing—presumably, there were more single-parent families, more poverty, and less reading at home, for example—and the school was not taking these changes into account in its methods of operation. The students whom the school was receiving differed in some significant ways from the students of previous years, and business as usual was not appropriate.

A further reason for change, as this team saw it, was the teachers themselves. New ideas to which the faculty was exposed made it impossible for them to be satisfied any longer with the ways in which they carried out their professional responsibilities. They recognized more than ever that their own needs were not being met. They were no longer happy with their traditional roles in the school.

Then the team turned to the question of what might be lost as the result of change. Much of what they feared had to do with giving up habits and the security engendered by those habits. They had found comfort in believing that the curriculum as it existed was appropriate. As long as they could cling to old beliefs, change did not seem necessary. They realized that it was reassuring to hold on to established values.

This team of elementary school teachers also worried that change would mean surrendering some of their autonomy. They had been able to leave the world behind when they closed the doors of their classrooms. Now they were considering intrusions—figuratively and literally—into their private cocoons. If they agreed to alter their teaching, for instance, it would mean an obligation to cede some of their unilateral decision-making power about what and how they taught. Also, the changes might mean having other teachers in the classroom with them—watching, offering advice, and perhaps even working at their side. Their time might not necessarily be their own any longer if they were expected to carry out certain duties on behalf of change. In this particular school, an aspiring professional development school that had allied itself with a university, they feared losing some autonomy if their partner in change—the university—ended up wielding power in the school.

Some team members projected further into the future and were concerned that they might lose the friendship of some colleagues in the school. After all, a member of a team who promotes change in a school, thereby attempting to make people dissatisfied with conditions as they are and asking them to take on new responsibilities, might, like Jeremiah, grow unpopular. They agonized over whether colleagues would still like them if they took on this role as leaders for change and put barbs on the seats of those colleagues. The team recognized that change would inevitably introduce uncertainty into professional lives that had been predictable, creating a situation in the school in which everyone might have to learn to exist permanently with ferment.

Team members questioned whether they had the competence and skills to lead the school through such unsettled times. At this point, in the midst of a summer Leadership Academy, they could not even be sure the team would remain committed to change during the long, difficult school year that lay ahead.

There were questions in their minds about the parents and the community. How would the parents react if the teachers were to proceed with the efforts they were contemplating? Children's education—children's lives—were going to be affected. Because the ways of the past were going to be discarded in favor of new ways that they were accepting mostly on faith, the team found itself uncertain about the curriculum itself, about how to carry out assessment, and about how to make the best use of time. And very important, they were uncertain about how the kids would adjust to the changes. Theories espoused by experts sounded fine in the summer, but once classes resumed, students would have to be helped to adapt themselves to unfamiliar classroom practices.

On a very practical level, the team from this elementary school was uncertain about the budgetary significance of the changes that they contemplated. In its own way, an academy is a fantasy island detached from the mainland of reality. It is a place where teachers are wined and dined and where grand ideas are sometimes allowed to soar to the blue skies without any ill winds to dash them back to earth. The prospect of having to implement changes within the parameters of a school budget was sobering. In addition, the team felt uncertain about the impact on the school of being flooded by student teachers from its university partner.

The team members knew that the process of change that they were learning would mean divesting themselves of some of the notions and practices of the past. Chief among what would have to be unlearned, they thought, were many of the beliefs they had held their entire careers about the role of teachers in the school, their relationship to each other, the ways in which classrooms should be organized for instruction, and the manner of grouping students. Also, if they wanted to teach for understanding instead of for facts, they said they would have to rid themselves of the idea that "right answers" were the goal of teaching and learning.

In weighing the fifth question, they asked themselves: What are we committing ourselves to? In the responses to this question lay both cause for optimism and a caution that the road carrying them toward change would be unpaved.

Change properly executed would mean a better school, and this was a motivation in itself. They saw themselves making a commitment to "build a new institution." They recognized, however, that it could be done only with sweat and tears. Changing would mean reconciling themselves to compromise; every teacher would be giving up some autonomy for the sake of a larger purpose. They were committing themselves to reflecting on their own practices. They sensed that the decision would be the beginning of lifelong learning that, by necessity, would be much more than lip service. They would be destined to live their professional lives with ambiguity. As they saw it, that was the price of change: giving up certainty.

——— 4

How an academy happens ———

The lack of uniformity among academies is striking and reflective of the fact that there is no single way for schools to build teams. The variety also reflects the differing objectives of educational team building. There are, however, some features that tend to be common to most academies. These elements are for the most part distributed in a somewhat overlapping fashion throughout the length of the academy, although there is a kind of sequence to their appearance in the curriculum:

1. Bonding experiences
2. Activities to impart group process skills
3. Provision of facts and information
4. Indoctrination to a point of view
5. Bolstering of knowledge about content and pedagogy
6. Hearing about good practice from practitioners
7. Learning about how to work with external partners
8. Formation of a vision and a plan for school improvement within the context of the academy's mission
9. Placement of one's own school and one's own role in the context of what is learned

How these elements might manifest themselves could be seen during the four-week academy for middle schools held in New Mexico in the summer of 1991. It began with a week heavily devoted to activities that got the groups from each school to start acting like a team (element 1). Much that the group members were called on to do required them to reach consensus, forcing them to divest themselves of certain individualistic traits as they took on the attributes of cooperation and collaboration (element 2). While this was happening, the participants also heard presentations on the subjects of adolescence, at-risk issues, and cultural differences (elements 3 and 4).

The second week concentrated on curricular and instructional strategies, including interdisciplinary teaching, block scheduling, and cooperative learning (element 5). Representatives of schools that carried out some of these programs shared with the participants their experiences in connection with some of these approaches (element 6).

The third week featured, above all, the idea of interagency collaboration. These teachers and principals from middle schools learned about how business and government agencies might work with them as partners to enlarge the possibilities of what the schools could accomplish for their students (element 7).

The fourth and final week was devoted largely to shaping the plans that the teams—and one would hope they were teams by then—could take back to their schools (element 8). In this connection, the teams also learned about how to work with their colleagues and win their support for instituting changes in their particular schools (element 9).

DEMANDS OF THE SCHEDULE

Academies are places where an abundance of articles and even books are distributed to participants. Some academies expect participants to read the material as they go along—or even in advance—and to be prepared to discuss them. At other academies, little reading is required, and the material becomes a treasure trove to be taken home, dug into, and shared with colleagues who did not attend. These are academies at which participants either go home at night to be with their families (a *commuter academy)* or use the evening for scheduled events or socializing, which are intended to enhance the bonding (a *residential academy).*

At an academy that *did* assign homework, participants filled out— on the final day—a questionnaire that was revealing in its findings about their attitudes toward homework. Fifty-two percent said that they got "too much" homework, 39% said the amount of homework was "just right," and only 9% said it was "too little." In other words, fully half of the participants thought the homework load was heavier than they would have liked. When asked, however, how significant homework had been in contributing to their learning at the academy, 13% said "very," 33% said "quite," 44% said "somewhat," 9% said "not too," and 2% said "not at all." Could it be that teachers, who themselves complain about students not wanting to do homework, are not terribly dissimilar from their students when they become learners?

This is not how it is in all continuing education programs for adults. For example, the short-term residential academies run by universities such as Harvard for corporate executives tend to bury participants under homework every night, and the discussion of cases the next day depends on having completed the assigned readings. "You would be very embarrassed in front of your colleagues from other companies if you had not done the readings and you were not prepared," a Fortune 500 business executive who attended the Harvard Advanced Management Program told me. One is left with the nagging question of whether too little is demanded of teachers at some academies, although the variation among academies makes it difficult to generalize. The academy of Trek, for example, includes case studies that must be read in advance to prepare for discussions.

However rigorous the schedule, much of the success of an academy—as that of any instructional endeavor—depends greatly on the facilitators and presenters. The facilitators are the people who keep the academy functioning hour to hour, day to day. They coordinate or lead many of the sessions, interact with the teams, and give continuity to the schedule. A presenter may make only a brief appearance, speaking for an hour or two, or may lead sessions over two or three days. But generally, presenters have no overall, continuing responsibility to the academy.

The chance to bounce around ideas and engage facilitators and presenters in discussion is crucial to the development of the teams. It helps participants to gain some sense of the authority they must possess to succeed as leaders for change in the school. To sustain the interest and enthusiasm of teachers who are being formed into teams—and to expand their knowledge and help them to be analytical—the presenters have to be chosen with care. This is one of the most important responsibilities of the facilitators, who usually oversee the selection of presenters. Teachers seem to welcome presentations rooted more in practice than in theory. They appreciate receiving information and materials that they can take back to school and immediately put to use in their classrooms, which amounts to a sort of how-to approach. The more unsophisticated the participants, the more comfort they find in presentations that follow this utilitarian pattern.

Such an inclination on the part of teachers is a challenge to the academy. School change depends on more than providing teachers with how-to hints. The professional consciousness of teachers has to be raised, and they need to be imbued with theory. They have to start thinking on their own about how to improve their schools, and they need a process for change to take and share with colleagues. Clearly, however, this goal must be balanced by recognition of the need that teachers feel for the practical and for the immediately applicable. An academy that tilts toward the how-to approach runs the risk of becoming merely a more elaborate form of the traditional in-service. Building a foundation for the meaningful improvement of the education of students requires going beyond the transitory and providing teachers with a theoretical base that promotes careful and sustained reflection. It is not simply a matter of teachers acquiring new skills but also of helping them to discover by reflection what they already understand and know how to do (Schön, 1991).

The constraints that school teaching places on reflection are well known. Teachers are so hurried that like parched travelers in the desert, they often can think of little more than slaking their immediate thirst. The reason the publication *Teacher* was launched in 1988 by the publishers of *Education Week*, a fine, comprehensive journal that covers news and ideas in elementary and secondary education, was that relatively few teachers read *Education Week* despite its merit. So, an attempt was made to package information in a form that might be more palatable and digestible for teachers.

Incidentally, it should be pointed out that the best of the academies strive, much like some schools are doing today, to avoid relying on lectures. Sometimes, lectures are the best way to present information, but academies often try to use experiential approaches and attempt to structure the work so that participants are called on to "create" knowledge on their way to gaining greater understanding of situations in their own schools.

The Need for a Flexible Schedule

It is difficult at an academy to satisfy fully the desires of teachers to have time to interact—beyond the scheduled time—with facilitators and presenters, time for personal reflection, time with their teams, and time with other teams. All of this cannot be scheduled in ways that will accommodate everyone's wishes. For that reason, academies may have open time in the schedule that participants can choose to use as they please.

It is not readily determined how much flexibility should be built into the schedule of an academy. The schedule may have to be reconfigured as it is unfolding. Participants often say they need more time to digest the rush of new ideas that flood them at an academy. Like standing at the base of a waterfall, the experience is exhilarating but may be as frustrating as trying to catch some of the cascading water in a cup to take home. Teachers want time to sip and savor their experiences. When they are hurried, they are overwhelmed. "I'm going to forget all this information before we get time to plug it in at the school and present it to the other teachers," said a teacher at one academy. Participants at another academy felt oppressed by a schedule that seemed rigid. They craved more time to digest what was being force-fed to them. When the facilitators realized that the teachers were overscheduled, quick action was taken and some sessions were canceled to create blocks of free time.

Facilitators have to be flexible. For example, a facilitator must be prepared to intervene when a team is struggling in its gestation as a team. Facilitators who tried at first to take a hands-off approach at one academy reevaluated this approach in light of the problems that members of some teams were having in relating to their teammates. The facilitators had thought that teams could be left on their own to wrestle their way through emotional difficulties, believing that adversity was a cauldron in which tenacity could be brewed. There is a point, however, at which infighting grows counterproductive and can imperil the possibility of the group ever functioning as a team. These particular facilitators eventually moved toward a careful, catalytic style of intervention, seeing that it was necessary to pull team members aside from time to time and lead them through mediation.

What this illustrates is that team building cannot be left to run entirely on its own once a schedule is in place. Facilitators must continually take the temperatures of teams. This interventionist approach was in evidence at a Leadership Academy in New Mexico at which facilitators regularly circulated among the participants, chatting with them about progress and problems. If one team member was not getting along with another, a facilitator seemed to know it and, where necessary, tried to help the team fashion a remedy. Those who are running an academy should make themselves available to the participants in a nonjudgmental way so that members of teams are inclined to approach them when difficulties arise.

Reflection and Feedback

There are various ways in which academy participants might reflect on their experiences and give feedback to facilitators. Some academies find it useful to ask participants to maintain journals in which they write each day. A journal can be used to record information and ideas that arise during scheduled parts of the programs. It may also function as a diary in which to keep personal thoughts about the academy and its implications. Typically, a participant is asked to find a period each day for making journal entries. Maintaining a journal prods reflection and provides each participant with a record that can be consulted in the future. Most mornings at the Trek academy begin with a warm-up during which participants write in their journals. A topic is suggested for the day's entry, but people may opt to write on some other topic that they find more pressing. Above all, the aim is to encourage reflection.

At academies in New Mexico, journals were collected and read periodically by the facilitators, giving them a window into the ongoing reactions of participants. This allowed for appropriate changes and interventions in the schedule. Carefully handled, this practice of facilitators reviewing journals can enhance the academy. It borders so closely on a violation of privacy, however, that unless done as deftly as it was in New Mexico, the practice could cause more problems than it prevents. In making entries into their journals, participants were guided by two sets of questions. One set helped them to think about recommendations to the facilitators for strengthening the academy, and the other set helped them to focus on the change process by urging them to think about the impact that their learning might have on their own schools.

Responses to questions such as the following were intended to guide the facilitators:

What additional information would be useful to you at this point?
What are you thinking in response to recent information, activities, presentations, or discussions?
What else would you like to learn about?

Responses to questions such as the following related the experiences to the participant's particular school:

What did that presentation make you think about in your school?
What does this information mean for your school?
How could your team utilize the information?

Another feature of some academies is a daily debriefing session at which participants drawn from various teams meet with facilitators to provide feedback. A schedule might be set up so that participation in the debriefing involves different people each day. The exchange is informal, and the accent is on candor. This is the time for participants to say what they like and what they don't like, what they would like to see added, and what they would like to see eliminated.

The daily debriefing at academies sponsored by Accelerated Schools lasts an hour or two at the end of each day's presentations. It starts with a session called Pluses and Wishes, which participants conduct while facilitators are out of the room. A list is made of the pluses— everything deemed to have been successful in that day's program.

Another list is made of the participants' wishes—what they would have liked to have happened that day and what they hope will happen the next day. The facilitators then return to the room. The lists, which have been recorded, become the basis on which to launch the debriefing, which traces the day: what worked and what didn't, what was clear and what was confusing.

PERSONAL EXPECTATIONS OF TEAM BUILDING

Participants go to an academy with differing expectations. What they derive from the experience depends in part on what they anticipate and on what they bring with them, both psychologically and cognitively. Change is a word that covers a lot of ground, and so it is not surprising that members of the same team may not have identical goals. Nor, given their diverse backgrounds, will team members take away the same ideas and attitudes. Team members generally are not even certain what it means to be a leader in their schools. The only model of leadership that most of them can visualize at the school level is a principal, and they know that that model doesn't fit what those of them who are not principals seek to accomplish.

It is clear to almost all participants that a desired result of team building is that the individual members of the team be prepared to introduce a change process in their school, assume greater responsibility for what occurs in the school, and deal with colleagues in new ways. Thus, it can be revealing to elicit expressions of their expectations from participants shortly after an academy has begun, asking each participant what he or she hopes, more than anything else, to get out of it. The range of responses falls into several categories. These categories usually have to do with experiencing personal growth, melding the team into an operational unit, influencing the rest of the faculty back at the school, dealing with negativism from the faculty, and improving one's teaching.

Indirectly, so far as teacher participants are concerned, team building is about helping them to improve their major task: teaching. Yet, this aim may not be readily apparent while participants are preoccupied with activities concerned primarily with their ability to function as a team. The team, for instance, must spend time learning process skills—the mechanics of the interaction that allows a group to function smoothly. This is part of being equipped for taking on new roles in the school. From out of chaos, the process skills can bring the order that helps get tasks accomplished. Ideas are not enough without the ability to implement them and win over colleagues. These are typical of the expectations harbored by teachers in the early stages of forming themselves into school teams:

- *Personal growth:* Academy participants are eager to get a clearer notion of the individual roles that each will play on the team. They sense that everyone will probably not lead or contribute in the same way. They want to hone their communications skills and fine-tune their ability to perform as role models. They think they might be advanced in this direction by gaining greater insight into themselves, and they expect that the academy will help provide this kind of personal understanding. Participants also want their experience at the academy to help raise their self-esteem.

- *Melding the team:* As for the team as a whole, the expectation is that the academy will help team members to identify common goals and transform them into a cohesive unit. Team members expect to gain the skills and familiarity with group process skills that will make this happen. They hope that they will learn to trust their teammates, expecting that this will enhance the team's chance for success. They hope that the academy will provide what is needed to build bonds, linking even members who are in many ways dissimilar. Also, they expect to emerge with a framework for team management and group problem-solving techniques.

- *Persuading others:* They expect to leave the academy with techniques they can take back to school "to persuade the naysayers." They want to learn how to change attitudes. This is seen as acquiring "strategies to help bring people from out of their safety zones." They think this means being equipped with techniques for involving others and for drawing them into the work of change. This implies, as they see it, that team members must learn to be patient and understanding. Finally, to carry through this mission of persuasion, they expect to leave the academy with a commitment by team members "to take the risks necessary to bring change."

- *Confrontation skills:* It is already apparent to the incipient teams that bringing about change will mean acting boldly and confronting people. They expect to learn to be candid in speaking to colleagues and even to be able to argue "comfortably." This means, as they see it, that they need to learn how to defuse negative energy and to initiate change in a positive manner. They expect to possess techniques "to facilitate deeper interaction among colleagues."

- *Better education:* Given the ultimate goal of better education through change, they expect to learn "more effective ways of relating material to students." It should be an explicit goal of any academy to improve teaching, although some of what is done in the name of team building may appear distant from this objective. But teachers who are on teams expect that somehow there will eventually be a connection between team building and helping students to get more out of school.

ANALYZING AND IMAGINING

A team's preparation for school change involves heightening its ability to recognize what is and what might be. This means reflecting on prevailing conditions in the school, analyzing those conditions, and envisioning how the school might be different. It is therefore crucial in team building that participants be exposed to the change literature and to new ideas. Their growth as change agents should be predicated on what this stirs within them. They should have ample opportunity at the academy to practice using the processes of analysis and envisioning what they hope to impart to the school community. A team ought to be able to capitalize on its experience in coming to terms with realities as they exist in the school. The team needs to gain a sense of where teaching and learning stand in the school. A person figures out how to reach a destination on a map only in relationship to the position that he already occupies. Otherwise, there is no way to determine a route.

Being Analytical

Despite the potential that perceptive teachers have for being analytical, they seldom seem to consider in depth the circumstances of teaching and learning in which they labor each day, perhaps either because they are too close to the situation and take it for granted or because thinking too much about it is depressing. But a team needs a reality base from which to push off in the direction of change. A reformulation of purpose and the creation of a vision consistent with that purpose is a key to restructuring schools (Schlechty, 1990).

It was this need—for teachers to be able to see beyond what they are already doing so that they can imagine something different—that prompted a California high school that was restructuring to delay its visioning until the faculty had some new ideas in their heads (Foster, 1991). The instructional leadership team at this school did some reading to gain fresh ideas, drafted proposals for a new organizational structure, and presented this framework to the entire faculty, which then broke into smaller groups to critique the ideas.

There are various ways for teams to go about noting the conditions and practices in their schools. At an academy for middle schools, for example, the teams were prodded to think about their schools by filling in the blanks on a grid that was presented to them. Sections of the grid were devoted to such topics as students and how they are grouped, teachers and their communication with each other, administration and shared decision making, special services, school environment, the needs of each constituency (students, teachers, parents, and community), and the structure of the school day.

On one side of the sheet, the team was to describe the prevailing situation pertaining to each topic and, on the other side, to envision the future with regard to each. The ensuing discussions among each team as it moved through the grid planted the seeds for forming a vision that could grow into specific strategies for improvement. For instance, when the team from one of the participating middle schools examined aspects of its environment, the following were some of the early conclusions:

- Environment counts in the school, but rooms are too small to accommodate comfortably the size of some of the classes that have been assigned to those rooms.
- Teachers don't feel that they have adequate support from the administration.
- Kids get the message that they are not welcome because there is only one bench available for them to sit on in their recreation area.
- What does sometimes making the library off-limits to kids tell them?
- When parents are walking in the corridors, teachers usually pass them without greeting them in any way whatsoever.

One of the best ways to analyze the school is found at the Trek academy sponsored by the Coalition of Essential Schools. A team uses two sets of "lenses"—the logical lens and the causal lens—as structures for conversation and planning. This approach provides an organized way for the team to examine its school and diagnose its problems. The team is expected to take the method back to the school and teach the school community how to use it.

The logical lens involves discussions of the logic that underlies and connects each of five interdependent facets of the school. The five facets are the school's educational goals, structure, daily experience, culture, and the nine common principles of the coalition (see chapter 2 for a list of the principles). The team also examines each facet in terms of what it perceives to be the priorities, assumptions, and compromises of their school as it has been operating up to that point. An exercise employed as an example to help teams start using the logical lens at the academy proposes, for instance, that they examine the logic of a school schedule consisting of seven 45-minute periods per day. In turn, the team considers the "priorities" for the school implicit in this type of schedule, the "assumptions" about learning implicit in the schedule, and the "compromises" in teaching that are made in having a schedule with seven 45-minute periods.

The causal lens is a method that the team uses to look at its school and devise ways to promote key conditions, events, and processes that, taken together, can be viewed as general causes of success. When these conditions, events, and processes—which have been identified in the work of certain researchers—exist in a school, according to the coalition, they dramatically improve the likelihood of successful change. The five facets are in turn examined in terms of the support they offer or the constraint they place on the conditions, events, and processes.

Being Imaginative

It is no small matter for a school to have a vision toward which it is continuously striving. The mere existence of a carefully formulated vision can be helpful at a time when so many schools seem to have no purpose other than being daytime repositories for youngsters. A vision can create a much-needed sense of mission for a school (Wilson & Corcoran, 1988).

A way to move teams toward a vision could be to encourage them to imagine that a vision has already been fulfilled and to ask them to describe how their school might then appear (Miles & Louis, 1990). Pretend, it might be suggested, that the school was just cited as 1 of the 10 best schools in the state. List what it is that the school has accomplished to gain such recognition, the team is asked. This approach could be helpful in getting the team to overlook obstacles that might otherwise narrow their vision. What must be faced at this point is the danger of imagination being constrained by the limitations of budget, personnel, regulations, or other obstacles. Teams have to think beyond these barriers.

Yet another way to bolster imagination might be for the team to develop a vision of what it hopes to get out of the academy. This provides the experience of visioning and helps them to focus on what they most need from the academy in order to work for change in their school. From the vision it propounds, the team might select four or five goals to pursue during the length of the academy. In fact, it could be helpful to lay the foundation for this process in the spring, before the team even reaches the summer academy.

When a team from a secondary school in Michigan was asked to formulate a grand vision that was unencumbered by limitations, and to set out, subject by subject, what each aspect of this vision might mean, the team imagined the school to be a place where the following conditions would prevail:

- Children's experiences would be a basis for learning.
- Teaching would lead to understanding for all children.

- The learning environment would be perfect.
- Cultural differences would be fully respected and diversity fully accepted.
- Issues of poverty, drugs, and teenage pregnancy would be addressed.
- Self-esteem of all students would be high.
- Continuing learning would be available for the faculty.

At some point, a vision should be honed to make it succinct and to connect it to realities in the school. Some experts say that the vision that finally emerges should be attainable, while others maintain that it is proper for a vision to be beyond the attainable or else it is not a vision at all. Either way, it is vital that the vision be fashioned into a statement to which all members of the team can subscribe. A good vision becomes a rallying post around which a team can assemble. Spending time forming a vision, as John M. Watkins, a consultant to the coalition, said to me, "helps you create the future rather than react to it."

Team building is enhanced when there is a commonly held set of values and goals to which members of the team can commit themselves (Deal & Peterson, 1990). Ideally, the team will be inspired by common thoughts of betterment, and those thoughts will be an engine to drive school improvement. Deemed by the participants as one of the most significant outcomes of an academy for middle schools in New Mexico in the summer of 1991 was the feeling, according to a final evaluation, of "a sense of unity and shared purpose with a professional group of educators" (Nordhaus, 1991b, p. 3). Each of the high schools with character identified in big-city districts by Hill, Foster, and Gendler (1990) had a clearly defined identity. A school's vision of itself and its striving toward fulfilling that vision can be a part of what contributes to a positive identity.

Involving the School Community

How much of the visioning and planning should be done by the team itself? There is a limit to what even the most sophisticated team ought to do on its own, regardless of how much legitimacy the team brings to the academy as representatives of the school community. If the team were to march back into the school with a full-blown plan, the rest of the faculty might take umbrage and feel no stake in the venture. A way to avoid this outcome is to regard the team's vision and plans as a point of departure for discussion upon return to the school, a device for engaging the rest of the faculty in an ongoing conversation.

What this illustrates is that a team has to be flexible with regard to its vision and the plans that it develops. An academy can teach a team how to plan for planning and can teach a process for teaching others a process. If a team has any hope of engaging colleagues, it must regard the work done at the academy as only a point of departure in the never-ending journey to school improvement. Not all leaders see their role this way, and as a result, intransigence can be a barrier to change. Charles de Gaulle exemplified the forceful leader. He had a vision for the France he wanted to see emerge after World War II, but he was inflexible and despised those who did not share his vision, which caused grief for him and his nation (Lacoutre, 1992). He seemed able to prevail with this authoritarian approach, but it is doubtful that many school teams could manage by fiat the way de Gaulle did and expect a favorable response from the school community.

When a school team assumes an authoritarian role and plunges forward without regard for anything but that which they have formulated for the school, it may be an example of what Fullan (1992b) calls visions that blind. Even the best of visions, after all, have their limits. "A vision not consistent with values that people live by day by day will not only fail to inspire genuine enthusiasm, it will often foster outright cynicism," says Senge (1990, p. 223). It is one thing to get words on paper and quite another to put flesh on a vision and breathe life into it.

Schools are filled with imponderables that complicate and confound the best of plans, so teams have to retain a strong dose of reality about what they are trying to accomplish. Planning fails partly because of the assumptions of planners and partly because of insolvable problems, according to Fullan and Stiegelbauer (1991), who warn against the hubris of the change agent becoming the nemesis of implementers. The authors caution that "the more the planners are committed to a particular change, the less effective they will be in getting others to implement it if their commitment represents an unyielding or impatient stance in the face of ineluctable problems of implementation" (pp. 99–100).

PLANNING FOR THE RETURN

Teachers who attend an academy want desperately to know how to share what they are learning with colleagues back at their school. The most prevalent worry among participants has to do with how they are going to win over colleagues to a new vision for the school. "We have strong personalities back there in our school," said a teacher on a team at one academy. "They will be wondering if we are going to try to force something on them. It's easy to be energetic about this experience we're having this summer, but then you wonder how you can do all this and still have time to grade the papers."

One cannot stress too much the extent to which participants in academies agonize over what they are to do when they return to their schools: about how they can ensure that there will be educational improvement, about how their nonparticipating colleagues will react to them, and about how to win the allegiance of those colleagues. They worry that other teachers will not be willing even to discuss new ideas, let alone learn and carry out new tasks.

A frequent shortcoming of team building is an insufficient response to this area of concern. Some teams get back to their schools only to find that they are unequipped to realize their objectives. Team building will have to give greater attention to this challenge if it is to become an enduring feature of school restructuring. Despite the high spirits and the many gains that result from an academy, it is not always clear to a team exactly what is expected of it or how it is to operate upon returning to the school. The members of the team have become a cohesive unit; their minds are bristling with ideas for their own classrooms and for the school generally. They have a vision and newly acquired knowledge of how to launch and carry out the change process, but perhaps only a vague notion of how to go about engaging their colleagues.

Even the doughtiest members of the team are apt to be daunted if the struggle must be carried out with little sense of direction and with few specific strategies. Look at what is happening in the former Soviet Republics for a hint of how much trouble awaits change agents when dissatisfaction is introduced without the accompaniment of attainable alternatives. As it is, team building increases uncertainty in schools. This is how it must be if team building is successful. The philosophy underlying the team's very existence is one that is intended to stir unrest by making people dissatisfied with the school as it has previously operated. It is this dissatisfaction and a vision of something better that propel the team and those whom they engage. Uncertainty inevitably thrives in such a milieu. Teams should be ready for this, but the uncertainty need not be exacerbated by a team not knowing how to proceed with its work.

The vision can be a cynosure by which the team sets its compass for the journey of change, providing a beacon to guide them as they steer toward their objectives. A series of short-range goals can be set out as buoys along the sea-lane to keep the work of the team from diverging too far from the course that will lead them to realization of their long-range goals. Some theorists define leadership in terms of its instrumental value for accomplishing a group's goals (Bass, 1990). The goals, short range and long range, allow the team to get down to specifics as it moves toward the vision. In their study of teams in many kinds of settings, Larson and LaFasto (1989) found that high-performance teams have both a clear understanding of the goal to be achieved and a belief that the goal embodies a worthwhile or important result, while ineffective teams have a goal that has become unfocused, politicized, or of diminished importance.

A central feature in the schedules of most academies is the planning that is done for reaching the goals. An evaluator at one academy concluded that team members "feel they need more time scheduled for writing and developing plans. Some also feel a great need for a break during the academy so they could either return to their communities to get input and differing perspectives or simply to rest and have a chance to process some of the information" (Nordhaus, 1990, p. 4). For this kind of planning, time must be built into the early part of the academy schedule so that the team may start thinking about its plan for the school. Planning time is likely to account for a growing portion of the day as the academy moves toward its conclusion.

TEACHERS AS LEADERS

Leadership in the context of team building means ending up being able to model for and/or engage colleagues. Teacher leadership can be a lever to pry the rest of the faculty loose from the status quo. Schools will benefit to the extent that some teachers are allowed free scope to fill leadership roles. Gardner (1984) reminds us that not all leaders are found among the top brass and that leadership also emanates from down the line as well. Whether an educator functions as a leader may have something to do with the person's willingness to take on greater responsibility than that to which he or she is accustomed. One teacher whose work was described in a study said that becoming chair of the school's steering committee and, in effect, being recognized as a leader in the school meant no longer being able to walk away from conflict and disagreement, as she had been able to do when she bore no responsibility for the school at large (Rackliffe, 1991).

Some teachers—maybe most—don't want the burden of bearing responsibilities other than the considerable ones they already have in their classrooms for their students' learning. Even in most teams that are trained at academies to go back to their schools and exert leadership, some people are better leaders than others and some are not leaders at all. An examination of shared decision-making programs by *School Administrator* magazine found numerous instances in which teachers were reluctant to participate (Goldman, 1992). A magazine for administrators may have a bias on this subject, but my own observations confirm a similar inclination by teachers. A qualification must be added, however, in light of research that shows that teachers appear substantially more willing to participate in all areas of decision making if they perceive their relationships with their principals as open, collaborative, facilitative, and supportive (Smylie, 1992).

The evolution of school change is still at a point at which many teachers are reluctant to step forward and assume expanded roles in spite of all the talk about teachers becoming decision makers. They prefer to work within the confines of their own classrooms to try to make a difference that way. They are willing to let others assert themselves and perform on the larger stage. This is fine. A situation in which everyone in the school was attempting to be a leader at once would be anarchic. Anyway, there can be no good leaders without good followers. What is leadership? Gardner (1990) offers a list of tasks that leaders perform:

Envisioning goals
Affirming values
Motivating
Managing
Achieving unity
Explaining
Serving as a symbol
Representing the group
Renewing

The team as a whole has to carry out certain tasks if it is to lead the way to change. If the right people are chosen for the team, some will have leadership potential and some are already leaders in the school, although they are not necessarily aware of the influence they exert. There was, for instance, the third-grade teacher in Michigan who said that not until she had discussions with her teammates at the academy did she discover that she was considered a leader in the school. "Never before had I thought of myself as a leader," she said of this awakening. One can conclude, based on the outcomes of the academies, that individual teachers and administrators may be trained to make contributions to their schools beyond what might normally be expected of them and may even be trained to take on responsibilities greater than those they might otherwise assume. When a survey in Minnesota asked those who had participated in team building to identify outcomes at their schools that could be attributed solely to the team building experience, the single largest portion of responses, 47%, included mention of "expanded leadership" (Minnesota Department of Education, 1992, p. 40).

Yet, one must be chary of such opinions. In recent years, a tendency has arisen to call almost anything extra that a classroom teacher does "teacher leadership." I have seen this label applied when teachers mentor younger teachers, when they cooperate with partners from outside the school, when they contribute to curriculum development, and when they assume any of the multitude of tasks they might perform in addition to their normal duties. Such activities are laudatory and tend to be above and beyond the normal call of duty. These acts may even be exemplary, but they do not necessarily signify leadership. It is demeaning to the work of true leaders to award the appellation of leader so freely. Simply doing something extra does not convert a teacher into a leader.

Similarly, there is an inclination to refer almost automatically to principals as "school leaders." The ready use of the title "leader" in this instance takes no account of the fact that simply holding a position does not make one a leader. This can be true even at the level of president of the United States, as was underscored in the debate during the 1992 campaign over George Bush's worthiness to continue in office. Managers may lead and leaders may manage, but the two activities are not necessarily synonymous (Bass, 1990). All principals are not necessarily leaders. Some principals may be excellent managers, but keeping the train running on time—as important as that is—does not have the same impact as redesigning the engine or charting a route for tracks to be laid in order to carry the train in a new direction.

Perhaps it is because of the scarcity of real leadership—both in the ranks of principals and among teachers—that the title "leader" is so readily conferred. Members of teams—both principals and teachers— need to have their horizons broadened at academies so that their view of what constitutes leadership can be more extensive. Scott D. Thomson has spent a career trying to lift the level of principals so that they might be leaders. He did that first as executive director of the National Association of Secondary School Principals and later as executive secretary of the National Policy Board for Educational Administration. Thomson (1991) offers a definition of the functions of the principal as a leader that could be equally helpful in considering the work of all members of teams:

> Define the purposes of schooling; develop the vision of a learning community; involve all stakeholders in the vision; plan, initiate, manage and evaluate programs to achieve goals; develop staff; anticipate and resolve problems collegially; carry through and evaluate and report outcomes. (p. 32)

5

Bonding and growing

As the curtain rises on an academy, the stage is filled with a cast of separate characters, each performing his or her own one-person show. The goal is to blend the various individual acts, getting them to mesh so that eventually the ensemble presents an integrated performance in which the roles resonate, producing a unified outcome. The fact that the members of the team start out reading from separate scripts should not be surprising, but if they don't get beyond that point, this will be a theater of the absurd—with everyone talking at the same time, no one listening, and the education of children unaffected.

It can't be assumed that just because some members of the school community assemble as a group in the sunshine of a new setting, the old issues and antagonisms will immediately evaporate. This is hardly the case. Rivalries, antipathies, philosophical differences, and all the factors that divide those who work together and impinge on their relationships with one another are brought along to a retreat. This kind of baggage does not get left behind. As a matter of fact, the openness encouraged by team building might raise the lid on some of the conflict that has been kept under lock and key.

The divisions of the past won't heal just because people eat their meals together for a few weeks and—if it is residential retreat—sleep under the same roof. In some schools, teachers are divided into factions and are not inclined to work together. There may be a need at an academy to overcome or at least neutralize hostility. Or it may be only a matter of dealing with personality differences. Schools, no less than other kinds of places where people work together, are very much affected by antagonisms among and between employees.

On the other hand, there is a reasonable prospect that when school people spend an extended period together in intensive interaction of the sort possible in an academy for team building, they may eventually begin to take on new feelings about each other. Former foes will not necessarily hug each other, but they may bond in ways that they had not anticipated. Shared experiences that are in many cases designed to promote bonding may provide a foundation for building relationships based on understanding and perhaps even mutual respect. Those who have participated in such experiences have seen this happen. It is easier to nurture changes in attitude among the members of a small, tightly knit team than among an entire faculty. The downside is that there is no assurance that the changes among team members, as profound as they may be, will penetrate the rest of the faculty.

The team grows stronger when its members recognize and acknowledge one another's strengths and understand and empathize with one another's concerns. This is the way to start stripping away defenses and melding individuals into a team. It is a foundation for trust. It also helps define the roles that individual members will play on the team, which will benefit from capitalizing on the forte of each member. The synergy gained through cooperation may accomplish for the school what never could have been done by individuals working independently. Honesty and trust within the team can lead to the discussion of issues that had been dangerous to broach. This kind of team building is unlikely to be fostered without the right environment. It is more than an intellectual transformation. It must be emotional as well.

One of the tensions in team building has to do with allocations of time: how much to give to cognitive matters of curriculum and instruction and how much to give to affective matters involving group relations. Some programs studied for this book virtually ignored group process skills while concentrating on issues of teaching and learning. To be sure, teachers can benefit greatly from professional development that concerns itself exclusively with the cognitive side. But the ability to operate as a team and the insight that leads to an understanding of the change process may not develop without proper attention. Good team building goes beyond the academics to tap into the social and emotional sides of the participants. If participants become bonded, it is not just because they learned the same facts but because in doing so they also shared experiences that were variously humorous, inspirational, upsetting, and memorable.

There is, unfortunately, no cookbook that provides a recipe guaranteed to produce a team that will without fail be sufficiently imbued with and knowledgeable about group relations and the change process. The chefs are still experimenting with this very difficult dish. But there are precedents for the idea of bringing people together and immersing them in experiences that will affect their interaction and their personal approach to challenges.

OUTWARD BOUND

One of the better known versions of this approach is Outward Bound, a program that puts participants in rugged settings in which they make discoveries about themselves and gain a new appreciation of the meaning of relationships with others. For instance, the white water rafting expedition that Outward Bound conducts on the Green River in a remote section of western Colorado calls for organizing participants into groups or, if you will, teams of about a half dozen, who share a rubber raft during the day and a tent at night. They must learn to work together in order to negotiate the treacherous rapids of the raging river, and they must contribute to the preparation of meals and the setting up of camp each day or else there will be nothing to eat and nowhere for protected sleep. The curious phenomenon that results from such an experience appeals simultaneously to one's senses of independence and interdependence.

There is a point during the trip when each person goes off into the wilderness alone for a period of time—a day or longer depending on the overall length of the journey. This is the time to cope on one's own. Even when the teams are together, there are many independent acts—such as climbing a rocky hill or rappeling down the side of a cliff—that each person must do. Everyone learns that he or she is capable of performances beyond those previously thought possible.

At the same time, Outward Bound is about interdependence, relying on others for one's welfare and being someone on whom others can lean. Even though one rappels alone down the face of a cliff, a rope that is tied through the harness around one's body is secured by a belayer perched at the top of the cliff, who literally holds the rappeler's life in his or her hands. Lessons in interdependence are taught tacitly throughout an Outward Bound expedition. Pulling one's oar takes on new meaning when threading through the white water requires those on one side of the raft to paddle furiously to shift in a direction that will allow the rubber raft to avoid a jagged rock. The knowledge that a decent meal the next day depends on cleaning the cooking utensils today and stowing the food so that it will not get soaked is a reminder of the fragile web of mutual support.

It is not surprising that many corporations send executive teams to Outward Bound and to similar survivalist programs. People whose jobs bring them together each day find new bonds of collegiality as a result of shared experiences that challenge them as a unit. At its best, the impact of such team building can carry into the workplace, melding individuals into a team. There is even an urban version of Outward Bound for tough city kids to let them learn a new version of independence as well as the lessons of interdependence.

Academies for educational team building generally have no rapids to navigate nor any rocks to climb, but there is nonetheless the need for teamwork. The goal of team building in a school community is to produce a sense of camaraderie so that those who work in the same building will be prepared to cooperate in new ways in the pursuit of common goals that will lead to better education for children.

A PROPER SETTING FOR TEAM BUILDING

A step toward cohering as a team is for a group of educators to divest themselves of cynicism about working together. As cooperation in the workplace is not usually encouraged or rewarded in schools, participants in an academy have to learn to relate to one another in new ways so that the glue of team building can take hold. A good academy, where there is intensive interaction, is a forum for such a transformation.

Whether the academy operates on a residential basis or the participants return home each evening, they should be treated with the dignity that is routinely accorded to businesspeople who go to conferences. The setting should be pleasant and comfortable, the food should be good, the refreshments should be plentiful, and the amenities should be adequate. Attention to such details helps put participants in a receptive mood. When they feel they are valued, they are more apt to accept the notion of being leaders on behalf of change. This might mean holding an academy at a hotel or a conference center, but it is not essential to have so lavish a setting. Successful academies have met on college campuses, where participants sleep in the modest rooms of dormitories, and at other settings that are not particularly upscale.

And so it was that one June morning of a typical day at a Leadership Academy in New Mexico, six groups of six people, each school with its own table, were gathered in a conference room in a hotel situated on a hillside in Santa Fe. Coffee, soft drinks, and snacks were readily available at the back of the room. Pads, pens and pencils, scissors, and other supplies were also there for the taking. Elsewhere on the grounds, to be used during the limited amount of time given over to recreation, a swimming pool and a well-equipped health club waited to be used. The pièce de résistance was the view from the windows that enclosed one side of the air-conditioned room. A panorama of the brooding Sangre de Cristo Mountains loomed in the distance under an endlessly changing sky, so beautiful and perfect that the scene appeared to be a huge Kodachrome slide.

Full involvement in the setting and with each other are important to the bonding process. Memories of shared experiences help hold the team together through trying times in the less glamorous setting of the school, long after the excitement of the academy has faded like a summer tan.

For this reason, it is important to recognize that allowing some people to participate in the team for only a portion of an academy rather than expecting them to attend the academy in its entirety may be disruptive to team building. Sometimes, however, there is no way to avoid having part-time participants. When this happens, the facilitators must carefully monitor the team and the part-time participants to try to minimize the disruption.

Residential or Commuter?

The intensity that produces bonding is usually more readily attained not only through full participation but also in a residential setting where people remain overnight. The alternative is an academy that teachers attend each day and leave in the afternoon to return home, as they do during the normal workweek. Versions of Rockefeller's Leadership Academies as well as academies under other sponsors, have operated both ways. The issue is how best to get a participant fully engaged. Deep involvement is less apt to occur if a person leaves the environment each day, goes home, gets immersed in responsibilities there, and then tries again the next day to recapture the atmosphere of the academy. Mood is all-important to team building.

In a residential academy, the tensions and pressures that come from living and working together without respite are part of the team building process, albeit sometimes with a bit of emotional pain. In one instance, a team nearly fell apart over arguments between roommates. But these strains, believe it or not, can be beneficial. The more intense the experience, the greater the chance for the team's growth. It is important that members of teams become comfortable in speaking frankly to each other and in hearing others talk candidly to them. "Healthy conflict provides an opportunity for growth," participants in a New Mexico Academy were told at the outset by Roberta Smith of the educational staff at the University of New Mexico, sponsor of the Leadership Academy in that state.

A commuter setting may be an arena in which much gets accomplished, but seldom does it surpass a residential experience in leaving a deep mark on the participants. Also, the logistics of commuting may detract from the effectiveness of an academy. In one instance, participants were drawn from many school systems over a large portion of a state. Some drove for as long as two hours in each direction, spending four hours a day commuting and leaving home at 6:00 in the morning. It didn't work.

A concession to the budget at a residential academy is the assignment of two members of a team to each room. Academies that I have studied seem to find little resistance to room-sharing from participants. Even sharing a room is a luxury to teachers, who seldom get away on an expense account. In addition to saving money, this arrangement can aid the team building process. A lot of pertinent work gets done after dinner at academies, and professional collaboration between roommates accounts for part of what is accomplished. At the Advanced Management Program run by the Graduate School of Business at Harvard University for corporate executives, participants have individual rooms, but a common lounge and bathroom serve a cluster of rooms. Traditionally, these have been called *can groups,* a scatological term derived from the fact that the group members share a specific set of toilets. The bonding of can groups is an important part of the Harvard program.

Despite the considerable advantages of a residential setting, both time and expense must be considered, especially if an academy is to last a week or more. The same amount of money can be used to reach many more schools if the academy is held on a commuter basis. Furthermore, given family responsibilities and other obligations, some people simply cannot be away from home for several nights in a row. As a result, residential academies that last more than a week are usually organized so that participants go home each weekend. An interesting twist on this arrangement was used in Michigan, where families were invited to join participants during the weekend that came in the middle of the two-week residential academy.

It may turn out that academies that build teams for school change will be most viable if they are designed for commuters. Whatever the disadvantages, it is simply less expensive and stretches money further to opt for a program that has the participants returning home each evening. Some of the intensity might be retained with carefully conceived activities. Moreover, in an academy that lasts a week or more, say, the budget might allow for overnight stays once or twice a week.

One sponsor found that a commuter academy worked best when all the schools were from the same school system. The participants then shared a common district culture, and many from the various schools knew each other so they already had a basis for further cementing their connections. In spite of the experience of this sponsor, there is considerable evidence that participants gain from their contact with teams from other districts. So committed to this idea is the Coalition of Essential Schools that it sought in the Trek academy to bring together teams from various regions of the country and then to have them visit each other as "critical friends" to provide input during the school year. Strong arguments can be made on behalf of an academy that involves teams from more than one district. But if more than one district is involved, it is probably best, as previously mentioned, that no one have to drive so far each day that energy and enthusiasm for the academy are dissipated.

Getting Away from the Hubbub

Whether the setting is residential or commuter, an academy gains from being held away from school facilities. First of all, this helps participants to avoid the temptation of going to their classrooms and attending to some of their regular school responsibilities. Also, it is preferable to use a locale that bears none of the symbols that overlay typical relationships in a school building familiar to the participants. An academy should be held at a place as free as possible from the trappings of day-to-day work, a spot where everything can be placed on a fresh footing. If it must be in a school in order to save money, then it should be in a building in which none of the team members work during the school year, and some touches might be added to make it less school-like.

Something is gained by having an academy in an isolated or otherwise deserted place, where participants can escape the distractions of the everyday world. This does not require a fancy conference center in the boondocks, but it does mean a place where distractions are minimal. It is much easier for a person to become immersed in team building when contact is minimized during the day—and during the night as well at a residential setting—with anyone unconnected with the academy. Then, even casual conversations will tend to revolve around the work of the academy. The informal interaction among participants is as important as the scheduled sessions in team building. Team building, after all, centers on creating ties between and among people; if the setting is not conducive to encouraging and promoting these links, there will be no functioning team at the end.

The impact was mixed at a residential academy held close enough to San Francisco for the participants to partake of the nightlife at Fisherman's Wharf and Chinatown. Enjoying the tourist spots together promoted a certain kind of camaraderie, but those who went into the city each evening missed interacting with compatriots who stayed behind. Also, they had less time to work on projects for the next day. Some revelers even had trouble waking up and staying alert during the next day's events at the academy.

Sometimes, even when there is no actual academy to help promote interaction, motivated teachers may instinctively seek to create supportive settings in which they can bond. For example, when a group of teachers at a high school in Seneca Falls, New York, wanted to talk about meaningful educational issues, they intentionally gathered away from the building—going after school to a local restaurant for drinks or dinner. This was not an isolated place, but being away from school ful-filled some of the same needs as an academy. It was neutral ground, not subject to departmental demarcations and removed from the pecking order that overlays interactions in the typical school building. Around the long dinner table,

> teachers from English, from music, from social studies and physical education listen to the representatives from the chemistry department talk about what it means to their curriculum to have their lab periods reduced. Teachers from physical education and technology depart-ments agree not to denigrate each other's agendas in their attempts to get rooms back from a plan that would collapse both programs into one room. (Grumet, 1991, p. 113)

The success of an academy during the summer appears to depend not only on where it is held but when it is held. Teachers usually don't like to break up their summer with something like an academy in the middle. Many participants say they prefer that the academy be held shortly after the end of the school year. It might also be useful to have it in August, closer to the start of the new school year but not so close to the opening of school that participants begin the year tired out. In addition, there is the possibility of splitting the time so that the first part comes soon after school closes in June and the last part comes near the end of the summer, although there are disadvantages whenever the sustained intensity of an academy is broken.

GETTING TO KNOW EACH OTHER

Members of a team may begin an academy almost as strangers. Some barely know each other although they work in the same building. Their contact in school may be fleeting and devoid of much opportunity to delve into ideas together. Their interaction may be limited to little more than an exchange of greetings and brief conversations about pro-fessional matters. There is probably never mention of dreams and ambitions or fears and failures.

And so, a part of team building is an attempt to get members of a team to become familiar on a more personal level, professionally and socially. Activities are designed to force people into contact and to compel them to let down their guard. This is done both within teams and among the various teams. One of the early activities in some academies is the administration of a personality test. The purpose is to help participants to better understand themselves and their team-mates. Taking the test and sharing the results are done in a spirit of fun and discovery, not to show that one kind of personality is better than another. Participants at one academy were intrigued as they recognized pieces of themselves being reflected in the mirror of a personality test that indicated elements of their personalities that were dominant, compliant, steady, or influential.

Forming Bonds Within the Team

An excellent vehicle for bridging personal boundaries is an activity, used at an academy in New Mexico, in which each member of the team is asked to draw a floor plan of the home in which he or she grew up and then to tell the rest of the assembled team about the floor plan. The exercise provides a window through which team members can get glimpses of each other's pasts. Surprising revelations emerge as each team member walks the others through a floor plan of his or her childhood residence.

Annie, as it turned out, was born and raised in Texas, where she lived in a home in which she shared a room with a sister. She never had a room that she could call her own until she went to college. The main way she could find any space away from others in her house was to go out and sit on the porch.

Sue grew up on a farm in Wisconsin. She found that drawing the floor plan evoked a flood of memories and good feelings that she had not tapped into for a long time. Her parents raised nine children in the house, which according to the floor plan was not spacious. She was actually born in the house, which had no plumbing until she was four or five years old.

Robert pointed to a room outlined in the floor plan of the home in New Mexico in which he was raised and said he always had a roommate: He was a twin, it turned out. His mother still lived in the house and continued to maintain the room in which he and his brother lived in just the way that it was when they were there.

Margarita's home in the barrio of a Texas town was an apartment attached to a modest bodega in which all the members of the family—there were seven children—were pressed into service. Her father was a carpenter by trade, but the work was infrequent; without the store, which operated from 7:00 in the morning until 10:00 at night, no income would have been generated for long stretches. Margarita was a shy youngster, she noted, as she remembered how much pain it caused her to wait on a customer, even to sell a pack of gum. There was no privacy for her until she found a cozy space at the back of a closet in her parents' room to which she could periodically retreat.

Brenda's father, a construction contractor, built the house in Mississippi in which she was raised. For some reason unknown to her, he placed the kitchen at the front of the house. As she drew the plan, she commented on how strange it was that her father had not situated the kitchen in some other part of the house. Hearing her teammates describe their houses made her feel very fortunate because, she said, she was an only child and enjoyed lots of room.

Carlos said his father had arrived in New Mexico from south of the border in the early 1920s. When he wanted to marry the woman who was to become Carlos's mother, he had to provide his future mother-in-law with references she could contact back in Mexico before she would consent to the wedding. The newlyweds moved into an adobe house onto which Carlos's father kept making additions, by mixing clay and straw with water to create the building material, as his family expanded. He even built a pool hall and a grocery store that he attached to the house. However, he didn't install pipes anywhere in the structure, and so there was never running water in the house. Carlos and his siblings were forbidden from entering the room he pointed out as his parents' bedroom. Carlos grew sad as he studied the floor plan, noting to his team that he had never had the parenting that he was now trying to give to his own children. When he pointed to his bedroom and the outline he had drawn of his bed, he said that he "peed" in his bed until he was nine. He said he learned no English until he was 10, a point at which he was required to attend a school with *Anglos*.

Through this intimate exercise, this group of teachers began to open themselves to fresh possibilities. They were being disarmed, letting down their defenses and preparing a foundation for the understanding and trust that promote bonding in a team. Throughout the duration of an academy, activities are geared to strengthening ties within teams. Often, teams are called on in the academy to solve problems, compelling team members to collaborate and to become aware of one another's operating styles.

Forming Bonds Beyond the Team

Almost all of the academies studied for this book involved teams from several schools and generally from several school districts as well. The University of New Mexico's academy is statewide by design and is held on a residential basis because of the vastness of the state. Most of the time during activities, members of the same team work together as a group, but some activities deliberately encourage cross-team participation. This helps build an esprit de corps among the entire group, much as the team will have to do with its whole faculty.

A benefit of contact with colleagues from other schools is the sense of becoming integrated into a network—a chance that few teachers normally have. Educators who participate in academies with colleagues from other schools can end up with a broader base of support in their work. Networks provide ties by which teams can nurture each other once they are back in their schools. In this era of telecommunications, innumerable possibilities exist for teams to keep in touch with and counsel one another. Networks reward participants with a renewed sense of purpose and efficacy (Lieberman & McLaughlin, 1992).

Therefore, the program of an academy usually includes activities that call for members of different teams to intermingle. One such exercise for helping participants to meet members of other teams is the collaborative school portrait. Each participant becomes an interviewer and an interviewee. A list prepared in advance tells everyone whom they are to interview. In a separate encounter, the interviewer will be interviewed by a third person. Thus, all of those from a school are interviewed individually by people who are from various schools. Then it is up to the interviewers, who did not know each other previously, to get together and create for the rest of the academy a composite oral presentation that reflects what they have learned about the school whose team members they interviewed.

At another academy, there is a facilitator who likes to use a game she calls the Last Straw. Participants from the teams are mixed into groups, and each group is given a box of materials containing old newspapers, masking tape, straws, string, index cards, markers, and three sheets of cardboard. The charge is to build a structure sufficiently durable to stand on its own that is at least three feet in height, is a thing of beauty, and is illustrative of the major principles and concepts of an Accelerated School.

There are many other activities in which members of different teams might engage to help them form bonds. The nature of the activity is not as important as the result: individuals on one team getting to know those on other teams. Ideally, they will stay linked after returning to their respective schools and will feel free to call on one another for advice and for words of support when the going gets rough. Sponsors may also hold periodic alumni gatherings so that the teams can renew contacts. Even if connections with other teams do not go beyond the academy itself, however, there is mutual benefit in the interchanges at the academy. It is just one more way that teachers in a particular school or school district can reach out beyond familiar faces and familiar experiences to speak with educational colleagues whose experiences either confirm or challenge their own.

GROUP PROCESS SKILLS

The effort to teach group process skills to teams is frequently not overt. Instead, participants are put in situations in which *they* have to develop processes for working together. Trial and error is a method of learning group process skills. Learning by doing has considerable merit and, like hands-on science for children, is an active and interactive process that may make more of an impression on the learner than simply reading about or being told how to perform some act. This is one of many reasons why an academy that lasts longer than just a few days can do a more thorough job of equipping teams with group process skills. Team building can be more effective when it lasts a week or longer. Participants need time to experience and reexperience group process, and they need opportunities to learn group process from several perspectives.

Barth (1991) points out that convening a group of people and sitting them down around a table "does not a team make." He explains:

> The formation of a school team requires developing group process skills in running effective meetings, in consensus building within the team and within the school, in securing and utilizing resources, and in developing action plans and evaluating outcomes . . . you must know how to work together; that is, you have to have the skill. (p. 126)

This is similar to what Wasley (1991) found in her study of three teachers in leadership positions in their schools. Despite the visible and potentially influential roles of these teachers, they lacked an awareness of how to approach colleagues and had little understanding of how colleagues would react to their suggestions, because these teacher leaders had no preparation for working in groups or for understanding group culture.

Team members at academies come to realize that a team's effectiveness is aided by the official roles that members might assume on a rotating basis each time the group convenes. The *convener* or *initiator* ensures that the group moves along through its agenda without getting bogged down and thwarting progress. The *recorder* or *summarizer* keeps a record of the deliberations so that something besides people's memories can be consulted to resolve questions about what did or did not happen. The *process observer* raises a cautionary note when acceptable group process procedures are not being followed. The *timekeeper* can monitor the length of each person's remarks to make it less likely someone dominates the discussions and to keep the momentum alive. There might also be an *information giver* to render facts, free of opinions, when such a resource is needed or a *tension reliever* to inject humor when deliberations tend to implode under their own weight.

The various roles are simply devices to get groups that are not accustomed to reasoning together past some of the obstacles that might otherwise obstruct their progress. Other techniques to enhance group process may be added as needed. For instance, some teams learn how to use the fishbowl as a part of group process. When this happens,

one group carries on its deliberations while others sit in a circle surrounding them. Like fish in a bowl, the group is on display as it goes
through its work. Afterwards, the observers comment on aspects of the
group process that they have just seen. Ideally, familiarity with group
process will facilitate meetings of all kinds in the school and improve
interpersonal communications in the building.

A presenter at an academy in New Mexico used the metaphor of
the juggler to demonstrate the importance to a team of good communications among its members. As in other activities, those at the
academy learned as they went along. They had no prior knowledge of
what they were expected to learn from the exercise into which they
were suddenly thrust. The presenter called on a member of one of the
teams, gave her three balls, and asked her to juggle. Needless to say,
the balls fell to the floor no matter what the would-be juggler did.
Then, each team was given a juggling kit that consisted of three balls
and a book about how to juggle. Team members were encouraged to
coach one another on how to juggle by following the instructions in
the book. After a bit of practice, a few people—with the instruction
and encouragement of teammates—gained a grasp of the rudiments of
juggling.

"What you did," the presenter said, "was different from what I did
in leadership style. I handed Margaret the balls and left her on her own.
It is a matter of one's style of delegating." This was, in effect, the para-
ble of the juggler—a lesson in how to delegate work. The teams were
made to realize that colleagues back at school might need help to carry
out tasks on behalf of change. They had just seen that with information and coaching, people had been transformed into jugglers. The
teams were reminded by the presenter that some people needed more
information and coaching than others. She told them that it was their
responsibility to make sure that those with whom they work get what
they need to perform the job.

E PLURIBUS UNUM?

When does a group from the same school become a team? This is a crucial question. Participants in academies often worry about whether the
team will be sufficiently cohesive to present a united front to the rest
of the faculty. They believe that any chinks in their collective armor
will provide weak spots to be penetrated by critics and cynics on the
faculty.

Probably, few teams evolve to the point at which all of the members subscribe totally to the same beliefs. This is not only unrealistic but
probably undesirable. A diversity of ideas expressed in a cooperative

and constructive spirit enriches the team. Especially as teachers' thinking on issues of teaching and learning grows more sophisticated, they are apt to have their own ideas about the particulars of change. Some will be more comfortable than others with ambiguity and uncertainty.

One of the most problematic aspects of team building has to do with its potential for bringing into the open issues that in the school setting have been assiduously kept under wraps. Among the most explosive are those having to do with race and ethnicity. Since a prime focus of some academies is the minority student, it follows that the closer that team members draw together and the deeper that they probe, the more apt they are to uncover sensitive nerve endings, especially on teams with diverse membership.

Reactions within teams can be sharp. There are, after all, discussions that touch on disparities in student achievement, multicultural curriculums, language, and the role of the home. It is entirely possible when candor prevails, for instance, that some teachers may admit they have low expectations of ethnic and minority language students ("Strategies for Preparing," 1992). Facilitators must be ready to help teams to deal with these touchy issues honestly and in ways that promote unity, not division. And once back in the school, teams must be prepared to confront similar reactions in the school community.

The point of team building is that members learn to work together, including being able to disagree without destroying the unity of the team. If they strive toward consensus, they can approach the rest of the faculty with some ideas that they agree are acceptable for moving along the change process in their school. As budding leaders, they may—stumbling now and then, of course—be able to rally others to the cause of change. The best ideas for improving schools are, after all, of little value if the school community is unable or unwilling to implement them.

6

The team and the principal

Much attention is given to the isolation of teachers, yet the isolation of principals is a condition no less detrimental to school effectiveness. In some ways, principals are even more alone than teachers, because teachers can do something to counteract their isolation more readily than can principals. A teacher is surrounded by colleagues of equal stature to whom overtures can be made. No such opportunity awaits the principal who wishes to escape isolation.

A principal, like the president of a college, has no colleague on staff of equal standing or equivalent responsibility in the hierarchy. Years of tradition have created a situation in which the head of a school or college has a special standing above the faculty, regardless of how many inroads have been made on behalf of egalitarianism. A principal who tries to reach out to teachers may find himself or herself in parlous circumstances. As the putative captain of the enterprise, the principal is perceived as being a step apart from the rest, someone at the same time to fear and to scorn. Overtures by the principal can easily be misunderstood and may make the principal vulnerable to rebuff.

When the National Association of Secondary School Principals sponsored its Model Schools Project, beginning in the late 1960s, the principal—as the so-called instructional leader—was to be the role model for change. The project revolved around principals, who met as a group and then went back to their schools carrying the message of change to their faculties (Trump & Georgiades, 1977). That approach reflected the prevailing top-down view in those days of how to achieve change.

It used to be that if changes were to be introduced in the school, it was the principal who was responsible for being the initiator. He or she was expected to engage the teachers, who were otherwise seen as spectators or passive participants in the process of change. Some principals continue to work this way, sometimes successfully and often unsuccessfully. A consultant to a New Jersey school that received a large grant in the 1990s from a business corporation trying to support school improvement found in working with the faculty that most of them thought that restructuring was the job of the principal.

Few principals, however, can take on the burden of restructuring alone. In the attempt to bring about massive change, it would be unusual for any single person in an organization to have the facts and the intellectual capacity to conceptualize all of the problems that must be addressed (Schlechty, 1990). It is not fair to expect even the most devoted and able principal to assume this burden. Furthermore, an approach of this sort dims the possibility of achieving success on behalf of students because it calls for dragging along the teachers rather than accepting them as partners. If teachers are not integral to achieving the solution, they are apt to be part of the problem.

This is in no way meant to imply that principals ought to be less important or less involved in the future. In most cases, even when individual teachers emerge as leaders, it is the principal who remains the chief symbol of the school and the top manager of change. It is just that principals should be relieved of the near-impossible task of having to change the school single-handedly. However, sharing authority with the school community is not a simple matter for some principals.

When principals join teachers from their schools as members of teams at academies, it is the first time that some principals have placed themselves in such an exposed position. The distance between principal and staff is narrowed as they participate in activities designed to meld them into a team. "When you live and breathe together, you are put on the same level," said a principal in New Mexico, commenting on the residential character of the academy. For the principal, possibilities of embarrassment are heightened. The hierarchy is shaken at its very base.

SHOULD PRINCIPALS BE ON TEAMS?

The most basic question about the principal in relation to team building is whether the principal should be a member of the team. A few years ago, as an observer of attempts to foster teacher empowerment, I was inclined to recommend that any activity aimed at enhancing the collegiality and esprit de corps of teachers ought not to be weighed down by having to accommodate the principal. My thought then was that teachers had to work on themselves and on their conflicted notions of professional self before getting entangled with the boss.

Now, I feel otherwise. The academies offer marvelous examples of team building in which teachers are able to attend to their own needs while having the principal in their midst. Furthermore, a team of teachers that returns to a school having forged a deep and personal relationship with the principal finds the cause of improvement immeasurably advanced. Some teams that are built without having the principal among them are continually anxious. Each time the members of one team without a principal at the academy tried to consider anything for their school that was the least bit controversial, they would turn to one another—with the principal in mind—and ask: "What would she say?" A principal in Michigan was emphatic on this matter. She said:

> It should be an absolute must that the principal attend. I didn't
> go the first year, and I always felt disconnected from the teach-
> ers who did. The next year, after I attended with the teachers, I
> felt a lot more comfortable, a lot more confident being part of
> what they were trying to do. I like to know what's going on in
> my school; I like to hear it first. It should be mandatory that
> the principal be there.

A principal who undergoes team building along with the teachers is more likely to end up sharing their convictions. "If I hadn't been there, I might not have been committed to some of what they became committed to, and they might have had a hard time convincing me," said another principal. In other words, the participation of the principal in team building is pivotal. When the principal is not on the team and the returning teachers must devote their energies to selling the principal on their goals, less strength is left for the activities of change itself. And of course, a principal who is not on the team is more likely to oppose the changes. However, a principal who feels at one with the teachers is more apt to be supportive of their efforts. The change most frequently noted by teams that participated in the program in Minnesota was the increased involvement of principals and the positive experiences that principals had as members of teams (Minnesota Department of Education, 1992).

Usually, teachers spend little of their working time in the company of the principal. Contact between teacher and principal is fleeting and often formulaic—prescribed roles at meetings and accepted procedures for reviewing teacher performance, for instance. There are few opportunities to be with their principals for extended lengths of time, considering the press of day-to-day work for teachers. The culture of the average school building is not supportive of the sort of informal interaction between teachers and their principal that occurs naturally at an academy.

Being with one's principal throughout an entire, unbroken day, as happens day after day at an academy, is a fresh experience for most teachers. Participating in situations in which the principal's opinions have no greater weight than the teachers' is new for many teachers—and for principals, too, for that matter. Such circumstances may even unsettle some teachers, as occurs when a child outside the home sees a parent in a submissive role for the first time. There is a tendency among teachers at an academy to defer to their principal and to anoint the principal automatically as the leader of the team. It takes time to break habits.

One principal—a strong person whose teachers were accustomed to taking directions from her—said that at the academy, the teachers continued during the team building to turn to her even though efforts were made to wean them. "The problem is that they will continue to think that I am going to call the shots no matter what we do or say here, until we get back to the school and they see that I am trying to share responsibility with them," she said to me.

Indeed, some teams leave an academy with the teachers and the principal still not able to accept one another as partners in the pursuit of school improvement. A school is typically a rigidly hierarchical organization in which notions of leadership take on trappings that might not be as readily associated with leaders in other settings. Positional leadership, conferred by virtue of one's spot in the hierarchy, is unchallenged at most schools, while personal leadership, based on traits that have nothing to do with the hierarchy, is not as readily accepted. All of this is to say that until teachers can learn to alter their assumptions about their relationship to the principal, they will continue to have difficulty imagining anyone other than the principal as a leader in the building. "When I think of a leader," said one veteran teacher at an academy, "I think of someone who has power and authority and is going to make me do something I might not really want to do."

Ties between teachers and principals are strengthened by the various experiences of team building. This is certainly one of the most important results of academies when principals are included on teams. The shared experiences have a bonding effect. A principal said that going to an academy with his teachers provided him with an unusual opportunity to interact informally with the staff for an extended period during which there were no distractions. Even the best intentions to do this are derailed inside the school, where teachers seldom stop thinking about what they will have to do next in the classroom and principals are beckoned continually by telephone calls or by the latest crisis in the building.

NEEDED: PRINCIPALS WITH CONFIDENCE

It takes confidence on the part of a principal to accept the idea of a team of teachers exercising greater authority. Not every principal is ready for such a change or prepared to be part of a team with teachers. It is important to begin from the proposition that some principals are more apt to flourish from the experience of team building than others. When a principal is insecure or caught up in defending the hierarchy, chances increase that the team's effectiveness in the school will be impaired. But other principals who approach their participation on teams with a sense of equanimity can win praise of the sort that one elementary school teacher had for her principal:

> He's changing a lot. And he's learning a lot, just as I am. He has changed his role. He never was a really authoritarian type of leader. Now, he has decided that the core management team is going to be the leadership in the school. He's told us that sometimes he can't decide whether the core group should do something or he should do it.

Clearly, adjustments in working style will have to be made if principals are to cope with change and retain their self-assurance while being on teams with teachers who have increased input into decisions. The principal's comfort level in accommodating change is important. He or she has to recognize that teachers often feel estranged when they've been given no say on issues that affect them and their students (Cherry, 1991). The challenge was summed up by a principal who went through a Leadership Academy with her teachers:

> I've yielded some authority. It doesn't bother me a great deal, but it takes a certain kind of person to do it. You have to be broad-minded. My role has changed, and the teachers' role has changed. My attitude is that if something is taken away from me, something else will replace it. I like to think we will have some exemplary teachers who will now do things for a broader audience. Some decisions are made now without my consent and even without my knowledge. When you first find out about that kind of decision, you think: Why didn't they check with me? Then you think: So what? I really can't worry about everything. It changes your role. When teachers become lead-

ers at one level, I have to emerge as a leader at a different level. You give up some of your autonomy.

Change can breed insecurity among less confident principals. It was not happenstance that when principals and assistant principals in Los Angeles organized themselves for collective bargaining in 1991, school-based management was being introduced and was upending much of what principals had long taken for granted. Fortunately, the threats that most principals feel to their leadership do not often approach what Gnassingbe Eyadema felt as president of Togo, when he was confronted with the idea of his subjects exercising greater freedom. This was a leader who allowed a referendum on his reign only after soldiers surrounded groups of voters who were given two cards, with one color signifying "yes" and the other signifying "no." The voters were told to hold aloft one card or the other to demonstrate approval or disapproval of their president. The soldiers all the while stood watching with weapons pointed, making sure that the oppressed citizens in this African country held up the right card (Noble, 1991).

The educational teams that turn out to be best positioned to bring about change as a result of attending an academy are frequently those at schools at which the principal—unlike Eyadema—was open and receptive to change and to sharing authority even prior to the academy. Find such schools and you have identified schools that are good candidates for team building, although even then success is not guaranteed. The principal of one such school spoke to me of what he saw as the inevitability of change once his team attended an academy. "Change will not go away," he said in acknowledging the determination of the teachers who were on the team with him. "There are now five people [the teachers on the team] who have been turned loose and given some of the reins."

Sometimes, principals lacking in confidence don't acknowledge their insecurity; this denial harms the possibilities of team building. "I don't feel threatened," said the principal of a middle school to which a team of teachers had returned from an academy that he did not attend. Pure braggadocio. He was scared silly. This was a well-meaning but ineffectual principal who felt under siege by teachers who wanted to make fundamental changes in teaching and learning. The poor man was in over his head. He seldom held faculty meetings in his school because he was frightened by the prospect of the teachers raising issues that he did not want to confront.

At one academy I attended as an observer, there was a team that had in its midst a principal whose body language sent an unmistakable message about how he felt about being there. Time after time, as the team was seated at its round table, he positioned his chair so that he was detached from the team, slightly turned and facing away from the team. It did not take a code expert to decipher this message.

In yet another instance, a principal who had attended an academy with her team scuttled their hopes and efforts once they were back in school. She would not honor the agenda that the team, including herself, had developed for school change. Pain and frustration seized the teachers on this team, and before long, they and other members of the faculty were petitioning for transfers out of the school. This was a principal who had felt threatened from the outset by the idea of sitting through an academy as an equal partner with her teachers. The team almost fell apart during the summer, and back in the school, disaster arrived on the heels of disaster. The team was quickly moribund. The presence of the principal on the team had turned out to be an assurance of nothing but grief.

A principal's failures as a member of a team serve as a reminder that some principals, like some teachers, are not only lacking in confidence but are incompetent as well. The difference is that an incompetent principal can have a more far-reaching effect on an entire school. A person who reaches this level of responsibility is difficult to remove. In New York City with its 1,000 schools, for instance, only one principal was dismissed during the entire decade of the 1980s, and the average disciplinary proceeding for a principal took 631 days ("Revised Rules," 1991; "Disciplining," 1991).

There is a need for principals—just as teachers—to have better preparation for their jobs. Being a principal is so much more demanding than it used to be that new consideration ought to be given to both the training and the qualifications. Once it was enough for a principal to be a caretaker, overseeing an enterprise that continued to run in ways that it had always operated. A principal's main responsibility may have been to perpetuate the status quo. Authoritarian gym teachers were often tapped for principalships. No longer.

Being a school principal is more difficult today than in previous years. Not only are the challenges greater, but the role is in flux and is in many ways being redefined as it is carried out. The best principal is now someone with the sureness to walk a high wire while displaying the deftness of a juggler. It was in light of just such new demands that the National Commission for the Principalship called for new standards of preparation and certification (National Commission for the Principalship, 1990).

NEW ALLIES FOR THE PRINCIPAL

Once back at their schools, principals who attend academies as members of teams find that they have at least some teachers on the faculty who can more readily empathize with them. This does not mean that teachers on teams with principals are—or should be—converted into sycophants or that principals can always count on the team members as allies. But it is safe to assume that as a result of going to an academy, there exists within the school a group of teachers inclined to give the principal a full hearing and sometimes even the benefit of a doubt. Said one principal:

> We can now have discussions in which I can say, "This is what I have to think about when I have to make decisions," and they will say, "Oh yes, we can relate to that." That doesn't mean they always agree with me or that they don't have their perspective and don't fight for that perspective. But they can at least see the other side now. They couldn't before, and it was adversarial sometimes.

The team in effect forms a bridge to the faculty for a principal who has shared the team building experience. Such a connection can help dispel possibilities of miscommunication and can provide a pathway for reaching the rest of the school's staff. This is not a matter of co-optation, and anyone who sees it as such is painting a cynical face on a well-intentioned process. Nor is this to say that there is no possibility of a devious principal using these ostensibly benign ties to teammates to take advantage of the faculty. It is best, however, to embark on team building in a spirit of goodwill and with an expectation of reasonable cooperation.

Another potential benefit of team building is the fresh willingness of faculty members on the team to accept part of the burden of leadership. These are teachers equipped with new knowledge and inspired by new experiences who recognize that with the mantle of authority come responsibilities that extend beyond one's own classroom. "The big thing that happens once you let teachers fill the role as leaders in their building is they stop using excuses for why they can't do it and start controlling their own destiny," a principal said. "It's been wonderful this year. I haven't heard the staff say, 'They won't let us.' They don't talk that way anymore."

One of the most remarkable examples of a team empathizing with a principal occurred at an elementary school where the principal had worked closely and effectively with the team. However, the point came at which the principal had to resign from her position because her husband had taken a job in another state. Distraught at the idea of losing her but cheered by their experiences with her, the faculty wanted to help her find a principalship in the city to which she was moving. So, faculty members voluntarily drafted a letter of recommendation on her behalf that she could submit to school systems to which she might apply for a new principalship.

In part, it said:

> She has shown courage and a willingness to grow during the difficult yet exciting process of determining our role as a professional development school. She has promoted professional growth by encouraging innovative instructional strategies, conference attendance, team teaching, and a full-inclusion special education program.

This was the ultimate accolade from the people who knew best: her teammates and their colleagues.

PRINCIPAL AS ENABLER

A principal who can help teachers to flourish, as this principal did, is an enabler: a person in authority who opens doors for others with less power so that they can make things happen. The National Education Association along with several corporate partners scoured the country during the 1989–90 school year to find 115 teachers who were chosen from among 20,000 nominees as being among the most exceptional in the United States. When the teachers were asked how it was possible for them to perform in so exemplary a manner, they said, one after another, that it was because they had principals who were enablers—principals who let them take risks (Maeroff, 1991).

Transformational Leadership

Principals who are enablers—the kinds of principals who help teams succeed—exercise what is sometimes called "transformational leadership" (Leithwood, 1992, p. 9), manifesting their power *through* other people, not *over* other people. A growing body of literature, as cited in *Bass & Stogdill's Handbook of Leadership* (Bass, 1990), attests to the power of transformational leadership to free followers—i.e., teachers on the faculty—to become leaders in their own right.

Outstanding teachers report that more often than not, their ability to sparkle is enhanced by a supportive and understanding principal. Such teachers tend to be risk takers and feel a sense of safety because they have principals who will not hold it against them if they fail while making sincere and informed efforts on behalf of change. These teachers find that the principal cushions them from the bumps in the rocky road when they take risks. In "good" high schools, teachers are shielded from powerful and shifting societal intrusions, and their autonomy is nurtured (Lightfoot, 1983). The liberating effect of allowing people to take risks shows up in many ways. When asked at the centennial of the University of Chicago to reflect on the factors that have made it the great institution that it is, President Hannah Gray said that it was the importance of risk-taking research (Walters, 1992).

Support from those in positions of power is of immeasurable value in bringing about conditions favorable to change. Academies for team building put fresh ideas in the heads of teachers and encourage them to try something new. Moshe Rubinstein says that a climate favorable to risk taking removes the fear of mistakes so that employees have "the responsibility to be right and the authority to be wrong" (quoted in *Highlights*, 1991, p. 2). A supportive principal who understands that some ideas proposed by teachers may not work or may take a long time to demonstrate favorable results can enable teachers to persist in the face of more immediate demands that others want to impose on them. Not enough attention is given to the role that principals and other supervisors can play as enablers when they use their positions to fend off intrusions that otherwise prevent educational creativity from blossoming.

Levine and Lezotte (1990) cite many writings in the literature that show that maverick principals who bend the rules on behalf of their teachers and challenge or even disregard pressures or directives from the central office or other outside sources contribute to making their schools effective. "Buffering actions of the unusually effective principal tend to focus on protecting teachers from external forces that threaten to reduce their commitment and limit their effectiveness" (p. 17), they say.

Novice teachers as well as experienced teachers notice the difference when they have enabling principals. One such beginning teacher, working at a high school in Massachusetts just after completing the master of arts in teaching program at Harvard, shared her impressions with other first-year teachers from Harvard. The teachers were linked by a computer system into which they were encouraged to enter any impressions, ideas, or findings that they wanted to share with fellow graduates. An electronic network of this kind is a marvelous device for breaking down isolation and building a web of support. The teacher said:

> I teach in what I would call a supportive environment. It is a working-class town, and we have approximately 700 students in the high school. Although I have had many frustrations with the motivation of the kids, I have been lucky with regard to support. From the first day of orientation, I felt like the administration cared and I still think they do to some extent. Anyway, my principal has been in to observe and offers helpful advice as well as endless encouragement and support for my

trying new ideas. He wants me to try new things, and I think he is there for me even if the ideas do not work. The same is true for my department head. Although we never have any really interesting conversations about education or teaching, she is supportive of my doing what I think is best. I have 100 percent academic freedom in the classroom. Finally, I attended an event one night, and even the superintendent came up to me, knew my name, and said some very supportive words.

At a high school in Pennsylvania that was eligible for a foundation grant being allocated for restructuring, the principal told me of being approached by a group of teachers who wanted to develop a proposal to bring hands-on science to the school and to link it to forms of alternative assessment. He immediately interceded to get them money to attend a conference that would give them more background for developing the proposal. "I couldn't give them the content knowledge, but I could facilitate their ability to get it," he said. "I don't have all the answers, but I can help them find the answers." He said he thought that many fellow principals were "afraid" to play this kind of role because they feared that their judgment would not be trusted and supported by the central office.

Thus, there is a substantial role for principals to play in setting the stage for the success of teams. Obviously, some teachers do well even without the support of principals. But given the contribution that a principal can make, it is good policy to encourage them to run interference for teams. Surely, one reason why more principals do not perform this function is that it can be thankless, offering lots of bruises and few extrinsic rewards.

One man who knew this well, both figuratively and literally, was Ewald B. (Joe) Nyquist, the late state education commissioner in New York State. While a student at the University of Chicago in the mid-1930s, before that institution abandoned the glory of football in an effort to underscore its commitment to academic excellence, Nyquist had the largely anonymous job of running interference in the very real sense of the word. He was the sturdy blocking back who enabled his renowned teammate, Jay Berwanger, the running back, to scamper to all-American fame and win the first Heisman Trophy. Sometimes, Nyquist saw himself doing a similar job as education commissioner many decades later, he said.

Backing out of the Limelight

Principals sometimes have to learn to retreat into the background, as Nyquist did, so that others can perform some of the acts that gain attention. One principal whose school sent a team to an academy talked of how he deliberately made sure that he did not overshadow his teachers when there were decisions to be made. He tried to become more of an observer—what he called a "process policeman"—offering few opinions but making sure that the right questions were being asked: What is bogging us down? Where are we on the steps to problem solving? "It means being much less judgmental and more descriptive, facilitating even to the point of partially not pursuing your own agenda," he said.

He was concerned lest the power of his position overwhelm the faculty, which a year or two earlier had taken the first tentative steps into the world of decision making. He elaborated:

> At meetings, when anything controversial would come up, everyone would turn and look at me. I knew I would have to look down and be poker-faced. After the first year, I could start talking because then people no longer expected me to make every decision. I had to be very controlled that first year or two because everything I said, everything I did, carried such weight, way beyond what it should have carried. People ascribe to this position all this power and knowledge. So, they would listen to me, even if I didn't have anything to say.

Another principal who wanted to bring a specific change to her school without imposing it said that she set out to get the teachers to embrace her ideas as their own. She regularly slipped notes and clippings into their mail slots to try to introduce them to the new approach that she wanted to see adopted. The teachers read about the concept, began talking about it, and eventually—convinced of its merits—took the initiative in recommending and implementing it. They had accepted it as their idea, and she was satisfied to sit back and not seek the credit.

It is not easy, however, for principals to operate in so retiring a manner. Some principals feel that they already have too little influence over a tottering enterprise and that to give to others the small amount of power that remains in their hands is illogical (Barth, 1988). What some principals on teams have discovered, however, is that it does not diminish them to find new styles of leadership that are more attuned to attaining desired results and less oriented toward wielding authority. The following are some of the lessons that principals say they learn by being members of teams:

- The role of the principal is not primarily to make unilateral decisions but to manage the process of decision making.

- The greatest obstacles to change at the beginning of the process are the people whom the process is trying to empower.
- Trust must exist in the school, and the test of that trust is whether it continues when things go wrong.
- Mistakes are an acceptable part of the change process.

There are limits on just how far principals should be asked to step aside. At the outset of one restructuring program, the mistake was made of directing the principals whose schools were involved simply to "get out of the way" and let change come from the teachers. This advice was well meaning but misguided. Perhaps there are some hapless principals who could best help reform at their schools by staying in their offices and keeping their hands in their pockets. It is not wise, however, to assume the worst about principals. In the district where principals were told to get out of the way, advocates of restructuring were still trying to soothe the injured feelings of the principals several years later. One wonders how much additional progress might have been made if principals had been enlisted as allies at the beginning.

SUPPORT OF THE CENTRAL ADMINISTRATION

It is not enough, however, for a principal to be agreeable to new arrangements for sharing power. Success depends on something more. The principal needs some assurance from the central administration that efforts in this direction are approved and even applauded. Principals, like teachers, need enabling. Deborah Meier (1991), who won national repute as head of an alternative school in East Harlem's Community School District 4 in New York City, said that it would have been impossible for her to carry out the work without the enabling strategy of Anthony Alvarado, the district superintendent under whose jurisdiction the alternative schools were nurtured.

On the other hand, consider the example of the principal who wanted to support a changed role for her school's teachers. The team had returned from an academy eager to continue its team building with colleagues and desirous of implementing significant change in the school. They worked diligently to bring improvement to the school. Meanwhile, the principal found herself walking the rim of a simmering volcano as she attempted to be supportive of the teachers. She was told in no uncertain terms by the middle-level central administrator to whom she reported that he didn't care about shared decision making and that she would be held accountable for whatever happened at the school no matter who made the decisions. She was given no incentive whatsoever to collaborate with the teachers or even to make any changes at the school.

In another instance, a district authorized six of its schools to send teams—including principals—to an academy, but the principals of two of the schools were reassigned even as the academy was under way. Then, in the fall, when there was a follow-up gathering for the six schools, an official at district headquarters directed the schools to send new teams to the gathering instead of the teams that had been built during the summer, thereby undermining what was intended as an effort to reinforce the existing teams. The official who issued this order had not been previously involved with the project, and it took intervention by the academy sponsor to get the district headquarters to allow members of the existing teams rather than new people to attend the fall meeting.

Team building for school change is not a practice to which most central administrators are readily able to attune themselves. Often, central administrators perceive their main responsibility as keeping order, seeing to it that the schools operate smoothly and without disruption. They expect the principals to harbor the same aspirations as central headquarters, and to the extent that any individual building deviates from the norm, it may be regarded as a problem school. Too much decision making at the school level may be feared as a potential source of chaos (Miles & Louis, 1990). In San Diego, the superintendent himself complained that it was difficult to build a broad-based constituency for change within the central office, where he said educational bureaucrats were comfortable with the old organization and its established chain of command (Jehl & Payzant, 1992).

The newly installed superintendent of a district that had sent a school to an academy spoke with candor about what the team from his school system would face upon returning to its schools. He said:

> You can't get away from the fact that as you try to change things, you will have people who are dissatisfied. We inherited a system going through political trauma. There had even been an attempt to recall the school board. Now, we have to get people to realize that change doesn't occur without conflict and that conflict doesn't mean that things are disintegrating. They have to come to realize that decisions should be made solely on the basis of what's good for kids—not what's good for teachers. There is a fear of change, and some of my administrators tell me that I am going too fast.

Bringing change to a school when central authorities have little or no commitment to the objectives is difficult. And although innovation might be introduced at the school without external support, the school cannot *stay* innovative without the continuing support of the district and other agencies (Fullan & Miles, 1992). In its national survey on the progress of school reform, conducted on behalf of the Business-Education Policy Forum, the Education Commission of the States found that the efforts of innovative principals were often being thwarted by district policies (Education Commission of the States, 1991). It is unreasonable for schools to be expected to make major changes—adopting site-based, shared decision making, for instance—in an atmosphere in which the central administration does not alter expectations and yield some control. The meaning of accountability has to be reconsidered, and the system has to see such change as fundamental and not as just a matter of tinkering (Hill & Bonan, 1991).

One of the many important findings from the middle school reform project sponsored by the Edna McConnell Clark Foundation was that the loneliness of risk taking for principals was reduced and that they were emboldened when they felt they had the support of headquarters (Lewis, 1991). There are many ways that superintendents can show this kind of backing. One principal who was part of a team developed at an academy was assured by the central administration that in the future he and his faculty would have a say in filling positions on the faculty as they opened up, which represented a break from the established policy of the central office to simply assign teachers to schools. A superintendent in the State of Washington, reflecting on his role in a district with seven schools, said:

> The superintendent sets the climate. The superintendent's attitude affects everyone. If a superintendent believes in an open system and communicates that belief, then the people working for you will have a sense of freedom and will become change agents for the teachers. It is up to the superintendent to do this for the principals. You encourage them to try and tell them it's okay to fail. The idea is to place them in an environment where they'll be safe to do that.

A possible method for getting more support from the central administration for team building is to have an influential member of the central administration go through the academy and serve on the team. Teams in the Coalition of Essential School's Trek are encouraged to include someone with "clout" from the district office. A superintendent can bolster the efforts of team-led change at individual schools by giving visible signs of support. This means, for example, that the superintendent—not a subordinate—attends important events and that the superintendent repeatedly spells out the vision for change and rewards those who respond to the challenge (Tewel, 1991a).

A superintendent who has the conviction to give this kind of backing to principals who are enablers must in turn be supported by those who can help shield the superintendent from criticism. The school board and the teachers' union, for instance, should let it be known they stand behind a superintendent who shows courage or else the person may not last long as superintendent (Schlechty, 1990). There was the case of an academy at which even the lavish and dedicated support of an outside sponsor, a foundation, failed to head off problems engendered by the fact that the superintendent of a district that sent several teams was distracted by a struggle with the school board to hold onto his job.

A Commitment to Continuity

Also important in terms of the role of the central administration is its commitment to continuity in both the principalship and the faculty at a school that is attempting to change. In the Edna McConnell Clark Foundation's Program for Urban Middle School Reform, there was the example of the district that ran a summer institute for its participating schools but very soon had "not enough teachers remain[ing] in each school to form a core group dedicated to change" (Lewis, 1991, p. 44).

A principal who has created links to teachers and laid a foundation for improvement should not be yanked away and reassigned without careful consideration to the ramifications for the school (Maeroff, 1988). As the team's work in the school is so acutely affected by the stance taken by the principal, the entire enterprise can be jeopardized when a principal who has bought into the proposed changes is replaced by someone who has no history of involvement with the team and what it is trying to achieve. The engine of change can lurch to a halt when someone who has no feel for the rail bed takes over the controls.

Principals at two of the participating schools were changed during the first two years of the Schools of Tomorrow project in New York City, which used teams to lead restructuring. One of the newcomers made valuable use of the team as a change agent, but the other new principal stayed aloof from the team and regarded it as a disruptive force in the school (Lieberman et al., 1991).

A team elsewhere had no principal when it was sent to an academy, but a central administrator contacted the team while it was at the academy and told it the name of the person being considered for the principalship. The team knew the person and objected to the choice, and it was assured that the administration respected the team's opinion. Someone acceptable to the team was chosen for the job and was even able to join the team for the last few days of the academy. Seldom do teams find such respect at central headquarters.

Team building is trust building, and it is difficult for the team to have confidence in an unproved stranger who takes over the principalship. There must be some continuity in the leadership, and whenever possible, most of the team and the principal especially should be left in place for a reasonable length of time. How long is this? No one can say for sure, but it is apt to be longer than a year or two. It is probably no less than three years and very likely at least four or five years. In the Model Schools Project of the National Association of Secondary School Principals, only 13 of 34 original principals were still in place at the same school seven years into the program (Trump & Georgiades, 1977). This degree of turnover could not have promoted the success of a project that so heavily depends on the principal as the leader of change in the building.

New Support Structures for Principals

It is clear that even when principals are dedicated to change and to working with teams, they need ongoing support for their efforts. The paradox is that sharing responsibilities often means more work than ever before for the principal. A good principal who collaborates with teacher leaders does not simply delegate and then march out of the picture. There will probably be more meetings to attend, more people with whom to confer, and a host of other new responsibilities. A principal on one of the teams I studied said, "It's a difficult job for a principal. Teachers get released time to plan and think. There are no concessions for principals." This is a role for which few principals are prepared, although they are increasingly expected to perform it.

Sarason (1982) goes so far as to say that not by previous experience, formal training, or the process of selection "is the principal prepared for the requirements of leadership and the inevitable conflicts and problems that beset a leader" (p. 161). Attention is starting to be directed toward what can be done to create more flexible time schedules for teachers, but less assistance of this sort is available for principals, even for those who are most deeply engaged with leadership teams. A principal who attended an academy as a member of a team said, "I just wish that all the kinds of things I'm trying to do for my teachers, someone was there trying to do for me as well. That's a very selfish statement, but it's true. There is no reallocated time for principals."

Principals who were members of the local school councils created by state law to oversee the operations of public schools in Chicago reported that it fell to them unofficially to educate parents and other team members in group process, collaboration, and decision making even though there had been some opportunity for councils to have outside training (K. Peterson, 1991).

The Principals' Center at Harvard University's Graduate School of Education represents the sort of program that can equip principals to work more readily as members of school teams simply by helping them to become better at their jobs. One of the center's valuable offshoots is a network of support that sustains principals in the face of difficulties. There is a premise here that principals who come to share a culture of reflection, learning, and cooperation outside their schools want to see a similar culture flower within their schools (Barth, 1990). A similar venture, the National Principals' Leadership Academy, was established by the University of Delaware in collaboration with the Education Commission of the States and seven states involved in the Re:Learning program of the Coalition of Essential Schools.

Support for principals in schools that are suffering the trauma of change should come in other ways as well. Academies for team building can help eliminate the isolation of principals. The principals who are members of various teams at the same academy discover that they have built a basis for networking with one another. Properly nurtured and adequately aided, this network can be a source of professional sustenance to every principal who has participated in an academy. Similar concerns led to the creation of a network of principals and assistant principals from junior high schools and middle schools in the 24 school districts in California's San Mateo County. The linkup was started in 1988 by a few principals who sought to overcome their isolation. By 1991, participation had spread throughout the county, and the group was meeting every Monday morning at one another's schools to discuss educational issues and professional development ("California Principals," 1991).

A goal, therefore, should be to fight the isolation of principals simultaneously on two levels: by bringing them closer to the teams in their schools and by connecting them to other principals who have had similar team building experiences. Even when teams take major responsibility for promoting change in their schools, the principal remains key to the process. The challenge is to create new leadership models that accommodate others associated with schools without stripping the principal of the authority to function effectively. In the 1970s, a cornerstone of school improvement was the oft-mentioned tenet that the principal must be a strong and able leader. That is no less true in the 1990s, although it is said less frequently. A school in which decision making is shared will heighten its chances for success if the changes occur without impairing the ability of the principal to be all of which he or she is capable.

7

The team returns

A team returning to a school ought to have some idea of how it intends to make use of the team building experience. This does not mean that plans should be elaborately detailed, but there should be a general plan of some sort and a sense of what the team intends to do to get change started in the school or to advance change that was already under way. The most successful schools in the Model Schools Program sponsored for five years by the National Association of Secondary School Principals were those that took extreme care in making plans on how to proceed with change (Trump & Georgiades, 1978).

Although the members of a team may not see eye to eye on every point, enough time should be spent in conversation to enable the team to reach consensus on its major aims. A divided team with members going their own ways is not likely to prosper. Inconsistencies among the members of the team may confuse the rest of the school community. Conflicting messages can lead to ambiguity, casting doubts on the team's intent and ability (Zaltman & Duncan, 1977).

The difference between a team that is open in its work and has a plan and a team without a plan can be seen in the results of a study that examined how teams trying to promote the career ladder concept operated in two junior high schools (Hart, 1990). In the successful situation, the teacher leaders stated their goals and discussed plans for change at the start of the school year. They regularly published a newsletter describing the team's function and offering tips to colleagues, and they conducted observation sessions. The principal treated the group as a legitimate voice of authority in the school. In the other junior high school, the team spent most of the year trying to define its role, and only one member ever made observations. The principal gave only lip service to the team's role.

On the other hand, it is not politic for a team to return to school with a blueprint so fully developed that colleagues think they are expected to do little more than initial their approval. The school community needs full opportunity to fill in the details and flesh out proposals. They need the experience that the team has already had of going through the process of analyzing the school. No plan is apt to succeed if the staff is not given a chance for input. Spreading the ownership will create more stakeholders to work for change. Clearly, a team must be flexible and adaptable in dealing with colleagues. This is no place for authoritarianism.

One study (Louis and others, 1981) points out a team's conflict between taking unilateral action and getting others involved. A team that keeps the decision making to itself finds it easier to cohere around goals, agree on criteria, and engage in speedy deliberations—all results that would seem to make it easier to achieve goals. Yet, the researchers laud the idea of the team involving as many faculty members as possible in the deliberations. This way, according to the study, there is the promise of spreading a sense of ownership and gaining wider commitment to the solutions, and there is the likelihood of the solution then having greater relevance to the needs of individual teachers. "The advantages of both alternatives are maximized," the researchers say, "when there is movement back and forth between the deliberations by a small group and the involvement of all relevant faculty" (pp. 187–188).

Team building can be a victim of its own success if members of the team end up feeling they have exclusive ownership of the ideas that they bring back to the school. A team's ability to spur schoolwide change will likely revolve around its capacity for extending ownership of the ideas to other members of the school community. A retrospective of the New Futures program of the Annie E. Casey Foundation found that the project was impaired by its failure to imbue those who worked in the schools with a feeling of ownership. In this program, aimed at raising achievement while stemming drop-out rates, teen pregnancy, and youth unemployment, too much reliance was put on a top-down approach that did not allow for sufficient input from teachers, principals, and school social workers (Deborah Cohen, 1991).

Increasingly, business, too, recognizes the value of getting workers to feel a sense of ownership, literally as well as figuratively. Companies with at least 10% of the shares of their stock in the hands of employees generate superior earnings and long-term gains in the price of the stock as compared with companies with less stock owned by employees (White, 1992). It is estimated that by the year 2000, at least 15% of the ownership in more than a third of all publicly traded American companies will be held by employees (D. Walters, 1992). Obviously, those who work in a public school can never actually *own* the establishment, but if they help shape the programs and are given more authority in carrying out plans, the results may resemble what happens in private enterprise. Educating the school community about the essence of change is vital because ownership comes with learning about the ideas (Fullan & Miles, 1992).

Heavy responsibilities fall on the team. Its members bear the burden of operating as change agents in two different spheres simultaneously. First, they are almost certain to bring back from the academy new approaches that they are eager to implement in their own classrooms. Second, there is also the work that each member of the team faces in trying to spread ownership in conjunction with promoting and assisting schoolwide change.

SPREADING OWNERSHIP

Often, a team finds it advantageous to launch its efforts in the school with an event such as a retreat for the entire faculty at the beginning of the school year. An activity of this kind lets colleagues know that something important has happened to the team and that the team members want to share their experiences. Also, this is ideally an occasion to pass the torch, trying to kindle among others the kind of enthusiasm with which the team members are ablaze. At one school, the team chose to hold a series of three mini-retreats, inviting one third of the faculty to each gathering, instead of having one big retreat.

Other teachers are the most obvious ones for the team to try to reach in its attempt to spread ownership of ideas for improvement. But those connected with the school in various capacities should not be overlooked because so many people in the school community, including parents, affect the performance of students. The Rockefeller Leadership Academies stressed that teams should strive to win the support not only of teachers but also of the support staff. Some teams reported with fascination that "even the custodians" were invited to the retreats sponsored by the teams. Extending recognition throughout the support staff was clearly something new for many of the schools. The teachers, both those on the team and the others, were impressed by the idea of providing ownership to members of the staff who are not customarily considered insiders: custodians, secretaries, and cafeteria workers.

At one elementary school with only 15 full-time teachers, each team member assumed responsibility, once back at school, for speaking in person to 1 or 2 teachers who had not participated in the academy. They divided up the school to reach the entire faculty. The aims in each conversation were to tell the nonparticipants about the academy and to indicate that their involvement would be welcome. There is a fine line to walk. A team wants to communicate with the rest of the school but shouldn't act like a group of colonists bringing enlightenment to the natives. If the team can strike a balance—and it is not easy to do— there are apt to be colleagues eager to hear the message and willing to become part of the continuing conversation. What counts most at this stage is that the momentum is sustained and that the involvement begins to spread.

The team can gain by capitalizing on any favorable disposition in the school community toward the team. Sponsors of one academy found that colleagues perceived members of the team as having been empowered and looked to them for leadership (New Mexico Academy, n.d.). At one of the participating schools, a teacher who did not belong to the team that had been built during the summer was especially open to the overtures of the team and sympathetic to its objectives. "If we were going to change anything," she said, "we needed a small team to get us started. After all, not everyone on the faculty could go off to the summer program. Now, they have a lot to offer us, and they are disseminating it. They've tried to be a central resource for all of us, and they've done a good job of it."

Form may exceed substance at the outset in order to draw attention to what the team is trying to do. Arousing the school community is a way to build the launching pad from which all reform ventures will blast off. It helps, however, to have some concrete results in order to win further backing. Visible, early successes help a team to build support among the wider school community as well as keep up their own hard work (Lieberman et al., 1991).

The idea is, ultimately, to involve the school community in framing a new vision of what education in the school ought to look like. Schlechty and Cole (1991), however, caution against seeing the task simply as a sales problem—as a matter of selling change. They say that overcoming resistance is not the same as creating commitment. This is a worthy admonition, but on the road to winning commitment there may be a need to find buyers for a new vision. There seems to be nothing wrong with selling the idea of change if it is done honestly as a step along the continuum toward gaining commitment to change. Lots of Honda buyers were sold on the car by a slick advertising campaign for the "car that sells itself," and eventually Honda owners grew devoted to a car that they found to be virtually free of mechanical defects.

What occurs when a team returns to a school can be viewed as the beginning of a never-ending conversation that, at its best, will become schoolwide. It starts primarily with the members of the team doing most of the talking, but it should evolve to include more and more people not on the original team—people who get involved because they come to believe in what the team represents. The longer it takes to expand the circle of conversation beyond the team, the slower the rate of change in the entire school.

Teams wonder almost always how fast change should proceed in their schools, and they agonize over the pace, whatever the rate may be. This concern is entirely understandable. Eventually, however, teams in most schools find it best not to try to rush change. "Maybe we were trying to do too much too fast," said a team member at one school midway through the school year. "We've backed off a bit now and are taking things in smaller spurts. The teachers were feeling overwhelmed."

How fast is fast enough when it comes to implementing changes? There is, of course, no single answer to this question. In the face of pressure to show rapid success, it is worth bearing in mind that one of the difficulties that plagued the early stages of the Casey Foundation's New Futures program was the emphasis on quick results. In hindsight, some of the planners felt that the program might have fared better with less rushing at the beginning (Deborah Cohen, 1991).

If the movement becomes glacial, however, that can also be a problem because momentum may be lost and frustration can take hold. It is up to the leaders to give the impression that change is under way—however slow it may be—and that all things are possible. One way that a sense of action can be fostered is by having team members continually disseminating to the rest of the faculty the information that was acquired by the team. For instance, team members at one school took turns over several months holding seminars and handing out articles about at-risk students. They also worked with parents and gave demonstrations of cooperative learning. Doing this had several effects. It reinforced in the minds of the team members the lessons learned during the summer. At the same time, it enhanced the standing of the members of the team as educators with special knowledge of certain topics. It was part of the effort to proselytize for change, and it gave a feeling of movement toward objectives.

Teams, however, may not be as prepared for success as they ought to be. It turns out in some cases that teams do not know what to do with colleagues once they say they are persuaded and that they are ready to get involved with the team in restructuring the school. This response forces teams to make decisions about how to deploy peers—decisions that some teams are initially reluctant to make (Watkins, 1992).

A subtle aspect of a team's impact on the school can be the introduction of group process procedures into settings in which they had not previously been used. When a group is operating well, it does not get work done by accident. There is a dynamic—a group process, if you will—that accounts for what happens. If the team building experience was successful, the members of the team have already learned this. Once back at the school, part of their job as leaders is to model group process for their colleagues. The manner in which group members interact with one another, the forms of disagreement, the allotment of tasks, the reaching of consensus—all are foundation stones of the process in which a group works.

PERSONAL TRANSFORMATION

One of the strongest and most likely results of team building is the favorable effect on individual members of the team. Usually, those who participate in team building are at the very least changed individually by the experience. This is true even if the team itself does not evolve into an effective unit for improvement. Once back in the school, team members tend to feel and act differently and are perceived in a new manner by others and by themselves as well.

As one elementary school teacher said,

> For the last few years in my own classroom, I have been trying to get some different things started, such as cooperative learning and integrating subjects so they wouldn't be fragmented. Our system has been very traditional, and I felt insecure trying these things. Even though my students were happier with the new approaches, I worried that their test scores might not compare favorably with those of the students whose teachers were traditional. So when I went to the academy, it was like everything I had been trying was reinforced. I thought, "Wow, I must be going along the right path."

Said a teacher at another school, "I think I have gotten out of my shell. I am able to state my ideas and be comfortable doing it. I gained a lot of self-confidence." Time after time, team members behave in assertive ways once they return to their schools. The shy teacher who kept to herself grows more comfortable being part of a group, the gifted teacher whose expertise was confined to her own classroom now shares it with colleagues, and the teacher who was just one of the crowd accepts responsibility for leading a task force and keeps the group focused on its aims.

Demonstrating the impact of team building on individual teachers are the findings of a report on what became of teachers who participated in the Leadership Academy sponsored by the University of New

Mexico in 1990 once they were back in school (Nordhaus, 1991a). The responses were uniformly positive in attesting to personal and professional growth. Teachers spoke of an enlarged understanding of the complexity and educational importance of cultural issues. Also, they evinced a greater appreciation of at-risk factors. Instilling such insights in participants was, in fact, a goal of this particular academy.

The extent to which individual transformation occurs was starkly illustrated at a school in which the team utterly failed as a team because it was riven with dissension that dated back to the summer. All the team had been able to do as a group was hold a successful retreat. Team members felt nonetheless that they had benefited individually from the academy. "I was redirected," said a kindergarten teacher. "Over the last few years, I have been giving greater thought to my personal growth and what I would like to do. It helped me get this all in focus, especially so far as my students were concerned. Also, it was simply good to get together with professionals from other schools and share." Her experience was typical.

Individual members of teams, girded by their increased knowledge and a greater sense of self-esteem, tend to be more willing to speak out in their schools and to talk about what is needed for change to take root and grow. They sometimes find themselves articulating the hopes and desires of colleagues who have not had the advantage of going through team building. The zeal they bring back to the school can prove infectious as it spreads among colleagues. Other times, however, enthusiasm can be a peak from which members of the team tumble to the depths of despair, disappointed by the rate of progress. "I feel driven to make this all happen," said a veteran teacher who was the member of a team at one school.

Not all members of the school community feel comfortable contributing to the professional development of colleagues. It places them in an unfamiliar and potentially awkward position. One would hope that the team building process puts team members at ease in this role, but some may never acclimate to it. Progress may be thwarted if the whole team has such reservations. Thus, members of the team need one another's support. "I don't feel too comfortable approaching colleagues with new ideas," said an academy graduate at one school. "It has been easier to do this now because I am a member of a team. If it had just been left to me alone, without the support of a team, I wouldn't have been able to talk to others about what I learned."

Whether growth by individual teachers who fail collectively as a team to have an impact on their school warrants the expense and time of team building is an open question. After all, personal transformation can result without investing in an academy. Thus, team building becomes problematic if its main outcome is limited to personal transformation and the school at large is barely affected. The transformation of individual members of a team is not enough in itself to lead to the improvement of an entire school if the attitudes, beliefs, and practices adopted by team members are not eventually embraced by others in the school community.

In their call for reconstituting society, Robert N. Bellah and his associates (Bellah, Madsen, Sullivan, Swidler, & Tipton, 1985) write that individuals who are transformed "need the nurture of groups that carry a moral tradition reinforcing their own aspirations" (pp. 286–287). Furthermore, the authors point out that to be truly transformative, the movement would not simply subside after reaching some of its goals. Such concerns are very much at the center of team building for school change and will determine just how far this movement goes.

Being Seen as Elitists

A source of apprehension for team members is the possibility of being perceived by colleagues as elitists. Those who have not had the advantage of the sort of special attention that has been bestowed on the team may be jealous. Henry M. Levin, director of the Accelerated Schools program, said that a problem of working with a team instead of with the whole faculty is that the members of the team are "seen as insiders who had a boondoggle."

Once the team begins propounding its newly acquired ideas, another difficulty arises as team members run the risk of appearing to be know-it-alls. To a certain extent, this perception cannot be entirely avoided because the team *has* enjoyed special treatment and may indeed *have* information not possessed by the rest of the faculty. It is always a challenge for those who know more about a given subject than others to share it without appearing to be imperious. Some teams in the Schools of Tomorrow project in New York City found themselves accused of being elitist simply because of their energy, activism, and team spirit—all of which team building tries to inculcate—even when they tried to make it clear that they welcomed the help of others (Lieberman et al., 1991).

A team runs the danger of turning its vigor inward and working on its own so as to try to minimize the negativism that might beset the team from the outside. "We've seen teams get so enthused that they get so tight knit that they become isolated as a group," said Mary Lillesve, staff development supervisor in the Minnesota Department of Education. This tendency is illustrated by the experience of a team from an East Coast high school in the Coalition of Essential Schools: The team went off to a summer academy and had trouble engaging colleagues after their return because, according to someone on the team, the members just kept the conversation among themselves.

The tendency to gravitate toward an us-and-them relationship with the rest of the school has to be resisted by the team. The aim of team building is not to create a new hierarchy in the building. Yet, the reality of the situation is that members of the team tend to see themselves as deliverers of information. They may be inclined to fill that role by resorting to the model with which they are most familiar: the teacher-student relationship. In turn, not enough may be done to respond to the concerns of resisters and to involve them in the changes, with the excuse perhaps that the team wants to keep "the process manageable by keeping the numbers down" (Watkins, 1990, p. 35).

Other teams, however, have sometimes deliberately and perhaps excessively downplayed their role so as to diminish perceptions of elitism. At one school, the team, which included the principal, decided that its initial presentation to the faculty of what had been learned at the academy would be done exclusively by the principal. The feeling was that in this way, the rest of the school community would be less likely to view those on the team as an exclusive group.

Danger of Burnout

Paradoxically, a peril to members of teams is that of being overly enthusiastic and taking on too much responsibility for being agents of change. When this happens, they find themselves devoting inordinate amounts of time to their roles in reform, restructuring, and school-based management; they expect great things of themselves and think they have to perform as superheroes to prove themselves to the school community. They feel an obligation weighing on them because they have been the beneficiaries of attention and considerable expense at an academy.

However, their ardor seems to make them more vulnerable to disappointment when things do not go well, especially if reversals come on top of early self-doubts about their ability to carry out change. They may become candidates for burnout. The process of burnout is not inexorable, but halting it once the smoldering begins may be difficult because burnout has a way of feeding on itself (Farber, 1991). Thus, it is important that team members monitor, counsel, and console each other. Even the goals the team has set may exert a certain kind of pressure. On one hand, it would seem that clearly defined objectives would militate against burnout by reducing uncertainty, but if the goals are too lofty and attainment is questionable, then worry over an inability to realize the goals may heighten the possibility of burnout (Friedman, 1991).

Teams in Minnesota were asked if there were a point at which they felt that they hit bottom, and indeed, the teams at 58% of the participating schools said that they had just such an experience. At the largest portion of those schools, hitting bottom was attributed to indecision over planning, designing, and implementing goals; lack of support; and limited commitment to the process (Minnesota Department of Education, 1992).

One would hope that the organizations that sponsor team building would still be active in sustaining and supporting teams after they return to their schools. Operating an academy during the summer is insufficient—no matter how good it is—if the team is sent back into the lion's den and abandoned. At least Daniel had his faith in the Lord to sustain him. A continuing relationship between the team and the sponsor is needed so that there is an assurance of support. A measure of team building is, therefore, the extent to which the sponsor maintains ties to the teams once they are back in the schools. The prospect of success is certainly diminished without this connection. In addition, the sponsor can lend succor to teams by helping them to initiate and to sustain a network of teams made up of schools that participated in the academy.

Built into the Coalition for Essential School's Trek is a component called "critical friends," an arrangement that begins at the academy when teams from three different schools are organized into a kind of troika. This is a device to provide the team from each school with informed, empathetic observers who can help them to focus on the issues to be addressed. The first presentation by a team to the other two teams is made at the academy. Then, during the school year, each of the three schools is visited by teams from the other two. The host school sets the agenda for the two-day visit, and together, the hosts and the visitors reflect on the school's progress. Questions become instruments for promoting change. Presumably, such feedback and support from critical friends who are going through the same wrenching process in their own schools make a team feel that it is not alone.

SCHOOLWIDE TRANSFORMATION

The advice given most frequently during team building when teams worry about how to have an impact on colleagues is that they ought to accept the fact that not everyone wants to be part of bringing about change in the school. The team is usually told to invite everyone to participate and then not fret when some demur. The truth is that the problem of the great uncommitted masses is not easily solved and that even the academies appear not to have found any guaranteed ways of winning the allegiance of the rest of the school community. This concern accounts for the requirement by some academies that a given percentage of the faculty sign a letter of commitment before a team attends. However, nations have set precedents by breaking treaties; signatures on documents cannot always be assuring.

"We got back to the school, and there was a brick wall," recalled a teacher who participated in an academy in Michigan. "They didn't know where we were coming from." On one level, the idea of not allowing oneself to be diverted by the nonparticipants makes sense. Realistically, teachers who are not interested in the work of the team cannot and should not be dragged in, although the door ought to be left ajar for them to enter at their choosing.

The point for the team to bear in mind is not to give up on the others. An experienced member of one of the teams involved in the Mastery in Learning Project of the National Education Association (NEA) recalled colleagues who "seemed to be saying, 'Leave me alone.'" This team member, reflecting on the experience, warned that "the tendency is to want people who don't get it to leave. But it came to mind last night that if the people who didn't jump on board right away had left, we'd have missed some of the best teachers we've got" ("Putting a Priority," 1991, p. 2).

Another experience from the NEA's Mastery in Learning Project led a participant to observe that "a far too prevalent misconception about school renewal efforts holds that substantive improvement is best accomplished in a school system through the involvement only of those who are 'true believers' in the proposed innovations" (Wentworth, 1989, p. 1). She added:

> To the contrary, it is unlikely that any significant, long-lasting change will occur—in the structure of schools or in the basic beliefs about teaching and learning—without the involvement of the entire school community. . . . Positive dissent is an asset; it provides a valuable check-and-balance to the potential excesses or insensitivities or simple wrong turns of those who are eager for change. Working successfully for school renewal as a total community—making sure to include those who prefer not to change anything—is a task that will challenge a group's keenest human relations skills and understandings. (p. 1)

The report on Schools of Tomorrow concluded that in terms of influencing the rest of the faculty, it is important that the team see itself as responsible not just for making decisions but also for learning from and speaking to the rest of the school. The study cited teams that took care to represent the various constituencies in the school by reporting to and carrying messages from them to the rest of the team (Lieberman et al., 1991). Having such people on the team goes back to the original selection process, as mentioned in chapter 3.

The reasons why some members of the school community choose not to enlist in the campaign for change are complex. At one school, for example, an older teacher who was wary of the team said, "I have done things one way—which I thought was right. How could I change now? It would be an admission that all these years I was doing it wrong." It is clear, too, that some teams bring some of the difficulties upon themselves. I visited schools months after the summer academy only to be told by some faculty members that they still had learned almost nothing on a one-to-one basis from team members about the summer experience. Their entire knowledge of the team's activities was limited to what they had picked up during remarks and presentations at whole-faculty gatherings. This, it would seem, is not enough.

Teacher resistance to the overtures of the team cannot be divorced from history. It ought not be assumed that a teacher who objects to change is a malingerer or insensitive to the needs of students. There is the story (Margolis, 1991) of the new superintendent who was frustrated by the open resistance of teachers after he proposed a new reading program for special education students in the district. It turned out that the teachers were committed to the old program because the results were better than those in any other reading program they had used. The school system had spent several years before the arrival of the new superintendent persuading teachers of the merits of that program, training them to use it, and developing individual objectives for each student. As Margolis asks: "Is it any wonder that they resisted the new program?" (p. 2).

The reluctance of others to aid the team's efforts may arise not from a philosophical opposition to the team but from a feeling that the team represents just one more salvo in the never-ending barrage of new approaches unleashed on the school. "As far as seeing anything really change around here," said a teacher who was not a team member, "I don't see all these big ideas taking hold. You get back in your classroom and have to deal with the mundane problems. The fact that there is a team doesn't change that." Teams in Schools of Tomorrow tried many strategies to involve the rest of the faculty, but got only mixed results, with many teachers remaining ignorant of or indifferent to the teams' efforts (Lieberman et al., 1991).

The extent to which teams can overcome the resistance of colleagues remains to be seen. Change is usually not introduced in schools in ways that take account of the inclination of teachers to keep doing that to which they are accustomed, and change is then thwarted by the tendency to change personally as little as possible, according to Fullan and Steigelbauer (1991). The authors suggest that change in schools must often operate on three levels: getting people to use new materials, to use new pedagogy, and to alter their beliefs. Teams have yet to demonstrate that they are capable of dealing with these matters on any large scale.

Strategies

In line with the strategy of keeping the team's work open so that those who want to join the action may do so when they feel ready, the hope is that colleagues who do not feel pressured may decide one day to show up and enlist in the effort. A team member recalled a teacher who approached her one day, saying: "I heard you talking in the lounge the other day, and I want to hear more. Does it really work the way you said? Do kids really learn that way? Will you teach me how to do it?"

The TEAMS II program of the Achievement Council in California has developed a strategy aimed specifically at spreading involvement while keeping intact the team that attended the academy. The team becomes the school site planning team, and it sets up a larger group known as the school site implementation team to accommodate everyone else in the school who wants to get involved. The larger implementation team has the job of developing and refining a five-year vision and a highly specific restructuring plan for the education of the school's students. The smaller planning team and the larger implementation team work together to put the plan into operation on a year-to-year basis that calls for an annual assessment of progress. Experience has shown that the implementation team keeps growing as more members of the school community join the effort.

Elsewhere, teams in some schools employ a strategy in which the members separate and each joins a different task force or committee in the school. If there is no such system of task forces, they help establish such a system. By spreading themselves around in this way, the team members ensure that there is at least one person on each task force or committee who can contribute knowledge of group process procedures and the benefits of a team building experience. At one school where this approach was used, team members chaired the task forces on which they served; at another school, they chose not to chair the task forces, playing out their roles less conspicuously and becoming valuable resources to the task forces.

Usually but not always, a team that uses this approach also continues to meet as a team. In some instances, the team and school governing council may be one and the same. Or the team may act mainly as an ongoing support group for those who attended the academy—a small forum to continue to explore and expound on ideas for change. When the team has the preparation to teach a change process to the rest of the community, that becomes the team's role.

Based on the experiences of teams from a variety of academies under different sponsors, the following are some of the main ways that teams returning to schools perform their role:

- By setting priorities so that all of the team's ideas are not just dumped on the school with no sense of what is most important
- By modeling the kinds of behavior that the team would like to elicit from colleagues
- By anticipating objections so that answers are provided before some of the negative reactions are registered
- By remembering that each member is only part of the team and does not speak for the team as a whole unless delegated to do so
- By taking every opportunity to share ownership with the school community
- By providing enough time for others to interact with the team
- By striving to get ample opportunity in the school's schedule for time to work on the change process with the rest of the school
- By keeping the school community informed about progress
- By being positive whenever possible
- By maintaining a sense of humor about what the team is trying to accomplish

Confronting Conflict

It is important to recognize that there is going to be conflict within the team and especially between the team and the rest of the faculty no matter how well a team has been prepared for its task. Conflict, it seems, is inevitable in such situations. In one school, the team ran into conflict merely in trying to get the faculty to concur on the color of the sweatshirts that the teachers had agreed to wear to demonstrate their solidarity. So unavoidable are conflicts of some sort between the team and the school community that almost every team in Schools of Tomorrow ran into problems with the rest of the school at some point in the change process (Lieberman et al., 1991).

Early in its team building, the Los Angeles Educational Partnership saw no need for teaching team members to resolve conflicts, but a session on conflict resolution was added to the team building when the need became more obvious. The ways in which schools are organized and the patterns that dictate the interactions of faculty members virtually dictate that there will be difficulties when some members of the school community take the lead in trying to bring about change. Even the old school-based staff support teams—an antecedent of today's teams—were considered to have within their stages of development a stage characterized by dissatisfaction. When they reached this point, members of the school-based staff support team grew frustrated, angry, sad, and discouraged (Stokes, 1982).

Today's teams that are built in academies may have similar experiences. However, team members are more easily able to get through the dissatisfaction stage if their training has made them adept at conflict resolution. "I now can confront one of my team members and be candid about my disagreement with her without having to worry about offending her," a member of a team at one school told me. She said that learning how to disagree and how to express that disagreement was part of the team building process. It was stated earlier in this book and it is worth repeating that changing the school atmosphere usually depends on altering the informal rules by which teachers relate to one another. They have to learn to accept advice from colleagues, which is not readily done after a career spent working autonomously and out of view of each other. They have to learn in disagreements to focus on the substance of the words and not on the personality of the person who is speaking them.

Struggles to resolve conflicts of one sort or another are widespread among teams that return to their schools after attending an academy. The team may in some instances barely discern the underlying dynamics that, like an iceberg in the Arctic waters, pose hidden perils. A team at an elementary school in Michigan that was stymied by insufficient progress turned for help to a university professor whose academic field was counseling. The series of meetings that she held with the school's faculty brought them closer to recognizing and coping with the factors that impeded progress. Much of the talk in the meetings that she convened revolved around matters of power and authority. People who worked in the school were helped to see that their experience in dealing with authority figures in their families shaped their attitudes toward authority in the school. They were told that their new notions of sharing power in the school had to be divorced from their orientation to the hierarchy that had previously existed in the school.

The fact that women made up almost the entire faculty added an overlay to the conflict, according to the professor, who said that women were more committed than men to trying to ensure that no one was hurt by conflict. Thus, like a family that wants to avoid confrontation, those in the school tended to eschew discussions of issues that could lead to conflict. Disagreement was not brought into the open. Anger was repressed. The ostensible absence of conflict in this school was in itself a kind of conflict. The avoidance of conflict was supposed to help communications but had the opposite effect: undermining communications in the school and preventing the resolution of conflict. In this respect, a school is similar to other organizations. A norm tends to arise that coerces people into hiding their feelings and emphasizing the rational and intellectual parts of their interaction. As a result, little experience is gained in being able to deal with the feelings that those who work together have toward each other (Argyris, 1962).

In a series of four informal presentations, the professor spoke to the faculty about the accuracy of one's perceptions of others, the differences between feelings and behavior, how anger could be used to improve communications, and why conflict can be good. Three major communications skills were cited in this school as tools that could be used to promote better understanding and ultimately to help overcome conflict:

1. Asking better questions in order to get more accurate understandings
2. Listening better
3. Being willing to be vulnerable by making "I think . . ." statements instead of presenting one's feelings as facts

Meshing Reform Efforts

One way that team building can exacerbate problems in a school is in failing to anticipate the relationship of the team to others in the school who are working on various reform activities. It is not unusual in this era of educational dissatisfaction to have several different programs designed for change operating simultaneously in the same building. This is not to say that there should be only one such program at a time in a school, but it does appear that those involved in each program should have some awareness of and respect for those involved in other programs. And there might well be a need to coordinate the various efforts.

Illustrating this potential for difficulties is a school in which a team that had attended an academy was trying to implement its program with almost no regard for a separate team of teachers who had been trained in a statewide program to support restructuring. The result was a highly competitive atmosphere, although members of each team ostensibly disavowed the competition. The number of teachers in the school was finite, and the amount of time that each had available to act as a change agent was limited. The upshot was that two well-meaning teams—each bent on reform from its own perspective—were scheduling meeting after meeting and driving the poor staff to distraction and, in effect, forcing people to take sides.

Sometimes, such competition can grow downright rancorous. At another school, an academy-trained team was locked in a fierce battle with teachers who were pursuing a different program for change in the school. In this case, anger erupted as the nonacademy group grew ever more resentful of the team from the academy and of what they viewed as an attempt by the team to usurp their authority in the school. Both groups worked diligently, but I could not help but feel that there was needless and destructive competition instead of cooperation.

In an era in which reform and restructuring activities are as prevalent as complaints about education, not enough has been done to foresee the impact of such competitive efforts. Coordination must be improved, and more should be done in a noncontrolling way to head off this sort of competition and lessen demands on the precious time of teachers.

THE ROLE OF FACILITATOR

In almost all instances, regardless of how devoted members are to the team, they can give only part-time attention to its needs and mission. The bulk of each person's working time must be given over to the kinds of ongoing activities that would exist whether or not there was a team: the regular duties of working in the school. What this inevitably means is that the tasks that have to be done to sustain the team and to move it toward its goals may be accorded low priority by the already burdened members of the team.

There is, however, a possible detour around these obstacles. It is the appointment of a facilitator who has the time to lubricate the machinery that keeps the team running. One academy sponsor—a university that was using the team building at the academy as a way to create professional development schools—provided facilitators who spent a designated number of hours each week in every school with a team. Mostly, the facilitators were specially selected doctoral candidates in education whose work as facilitators amounted to research assistantships for which they were paid.

Typically, in this sort of arrangement, the facilitator attends the team's meetings, confers individually with team members, meets with other members of the school community about the team's agenda, and lends a hand to the principal in light of the extra work that the principal has as a team member. In addition—and some might say most importantly—the facilitator ferrets out the resources, both human and material, that the team needs. If the program is connected with a university, this might frequently entail recruiting appropriate faculty members to come to the school to consult with team members on specific issues. There are many advantages to having outside sponsors involved in facilitating the work of teams in schools. The independence and flexibility of a sponsor with links outside the school and beyond the heavy hand of the school system can help overcome bureaucratic obstacles (Maeroff, 1988). Assistance from the outside was deemed crucial in implementing a new science curriculum at schools in England. "An external change agent who could act immediately so that the difficulty was never left to get in the way of a major development ensured continuation" (Pennell & Alexander, 1991, p. 5).

Other programs to support teams tend—to the extent that there are facilitators—to use people whose time for the team is more limited. In Accelerated Schools, for instance, the school district is expected to assign two "coaches" to visit participating schools once a week. In the Minnesota program, a local coordinator employed by the school district provides support to teams. The amount of time that the coordinator is able to give varies among districts throughout the state. Help is also available to teams in Minnesota from the state.

In Panasonic Foundation's Partners in Restructuring Schools program for restructuring schools, consultants were made available at the request of the schools. These were mainly teachers and administrators from other districts. Schools tended to take advantage of this assistance about once a week. The consultants provided suggestions and ideas and helped focus the debate, sometimes merely trying to ensure that the right questions were raised in the schools. In addition, the foundation's own core staff "hovered" around the participating schools, dropping in to see how things were going, offering support and encouragement, and following up with phone calls (Holzman & Tewel, 1992). Panasonic, however, did not assign consultants to participating schools on an ongoing basis, taking the position that the extensive availability of a consultant would make it less likely that the school community itself would take the initiative in solving problems.

Although access to a facilitator may indeed give members of the school community an excuse for not finding solutions on their own, experience has shown that a good facilitator tries to be a catalyst, not a surrogate problem solver. This approach was illustrated by one of the facilitators assigned to a professional development school in Michigan. A professor at Michigan State University who was familiar with her work described it this way:

> She has a good touch with the faculty and lets them muddle through, not marching them through. She believes it is important to let them define the problem and to gradually interact with each other as they feel safe enough to do so. From the outside, it may look like a slow process and not coherent. They

started where they wanted and moved at their own rate. They could then contribute to the conversations by talking about their own thing.

I asked a principal who was on a team in a school that had the benefit of a facilitator paid by the university sponsor what the result would be if her school and its team were trying to change without the facilitator and without the university connection. "All we could do then would be to think about it," she said without hesitation. She continued:

> We wouldn't even have the reallocated time, and I don't think the teachers would have the knowledge base or the resources to do what has to be done. We couldn't get these good people coming into the school to help us without the university connection. And without the facilitator as a liaison, I don't think anyone here would have the time to be in touch with the university to discuss what kind of help we need. We would be left to do only the little things that we used to do, and that wouldn't produce significant change.

Some facilitators are less effective than others. A facilitator at one school I visited failed to win the confidence of the teachers and was more of a detriment than a boon. In general, though, the availability of a facilitator is of significant worth to a team. Some sponsors of team building do not recognize this, and some of the sponsors who do acknowledge the value of a facilitator find that they nonetheless cannot afford the expense.

Various strategies are tried. Sometimes, sponsors propose that a member of the team also act as the facilitator. However, extra time is not necessarily made available for the team member to perform this role. Furthermore, at best, a team member who doubles as facilitator lacks the dispassionate neutrality of an outsider, which is a quality that enhances the effectiveness of facilitators who are not a part of the regular staff. In one program, people such as state education department personnel are assigned as facilitators to help teams that attended academies. But, the state personnel are allowed only enough time to be able to visit each school less than once a month. Another sponsor unrealistically assigns one person to be a facilitator for teams at 20 schools.

Whatever approach is taken, team building will be incomplete without adequate facilitation for the team once it is back in the school. This is an aspect of team building that must get more attention or else investments in team building may be jeopardized.

8

Making time for teams

Teachers never have enough time. The constraints imposed by the clock and the calendar are enormous. What this means in practice is that every activity except being in the classroom with one's students must get low priority. And because there are a couple of dozen children in the average classroom, most teachers find that their working day has room for little else than dealing with the immediate needs of students. Of course, students *should* get the highest priority, but schedules ought to be designed so that teachers do not always have to give short shrift to professional development.

Teacher professionalism and all that it implies cannot flourish under existing circumstances. If teams and their members are to have an impact, there must be time for them to carry out their work. How, for instance, can a teacher assert leadership when the teacher can hardly get away from her students? How can there be time to explore and to develop mechanisms for change when a teacher is always teaching? As one teacher pointed out, "During the school day, you can really get eaten up by the daily management kinds of things and the daily teaching."

Another teacher, Sharon Harper (1991), who teaches gifted children in Wellsburg, West Virginia, was asked about the prospect of involving experienced teachers in the hiring of new teachers. The question tapped into some deep concerns of hers:

> What teacher has the time to hire teachers? I have yet to hear any teacher say, "I have so much extra time on my hands. I'm weeks ahead with my lesson plans. I'm caught up on my paper grading. I've sent little notes to all my students to raise their self-esteem. I've called several parents to discuss home reinforcement. . . ." The truth is that no teacher ever has enough time for adequate classroom preparation, peer interaction or—most important—instruction. (p. 31)

Trying to document the problem of insufficient time, a high school English teacher devised a formula for determining a teacher's total work time and applied it to a hypothetical situation in which a teacher has 150 students in his various classes. He took into consideration preparation for class, follow-up activities, and such tasks as meeting with students, phoning parents, working with colleagues, maintaining the classroom, handling attendance chores, and dealing with occasional responsibilities such as giving attention to special students, overseeing occasional class projects and trips, keeping up bulletin boards, and doing chores associated with starting and ending the school year. He estimated that on average, stretched over the school year and then broken down week by week, these responsibilities consume 43 to 55 hours per week. This time comes on top of at least 24 hours a week of classes, producing a total workweek of 67 to 79 hours (Bolmer, 1991).

In what other field are professionals called on to assume responsibilities for such menial tasks as enforcing order in lavatories, supervising traffic in corridors, patrolling playgrounds, and overseeing lunchrooms? The time squeeze is a main source of demoralization for teachers. It causes stress and breeds apathy, leading to burnout. Without adequate time, there cannot be proper professional development. Groups of teachers cannot find common time for ongoing planning and discussion, and opportunities are few for teachers who are serious about wanting to critique and study their own work (Wiggins, 1990). Teachers need time for individual growth, for collaboration, and for observation of each other, not to mention preparation for instruction.

Think of the differences between the assignments of those who teach in colleges and those at elementary and secondary schools. It is an unusual college teacher who spends more than 12 to 15 hours a week in classes with students, and for many the schedule calls for no more than six or nine hours in class. A schoolteacher logs in at least two to three times as much class time as a professor and must devote as much or more time to preparation and marking of papers. Many college teachers spend out-of-class time meeting with students and attending meetings, but so do schoolteachers. Supposedly, college faculty members need schedules that afford them time to conduct research and write about it, but the fact is that such activities are carried out in a significant way by only a fraction of those who teach in the ranks of higher education.

NEW SCHEDULES FOR NEW RESPONSIBILITIES

Yet, the notion persists that schoolteachers, if they choose, have the time to contribute to educational improvement individually and in teams. Frequently, however, this is simply not so. School-based management and shared decision making are apparently supposed to happen without the investment of additional time for either training people for these new roles or for allowing them to deliberate over the decisions they are expected to make (Lindquist & Mauriel, 1989). Limited time can be a major barrier to informed decisions (Lockwood, 1992). Teams that participated in the Minnesota Educational Effectiveness Program said that the least change came in terms of needed allocations of time and money (Minnesota Department of Education, 1992). An earlier evaluation in Minnesota found that among schools that reduced or eliminated their participation in the improvement program, the primary reasons for doing so had to do with lack of time and insufficient support from the district administration (Minnesota Department of Education, 1991).

Different sorts of schedules for teachers are needed if, besides their usual work load, they are expected to take on the activities proposed under restructuring. Teachers do not have the time to prepare for change, let alone implement it. "When the rhetoric of restructuring meets the reality of daily life in schools, it collides with the problem of time," said teacher-education experts at Michigan State University in identifying time limitations on teachers as a main obstacle to creating professional development schools ("Making Time," 1990, p. 4).

Exemplifying this problem was the foray into site-based management by the Dade County schools in Florida. A tight budget robbed the schools of professional time that might have been given over to the cadres or teams entrusted with management activities, and so the groups often found themselves meeting on their own time. Furthermore, from the beginning of the program, adequate time for training the members of the cadres in management procedures was not available. Lack of time was almost certainly a deterrent to the half of the system's 300 schools that did not opt to join site-based management.

Similarly, time was the commodity most keenly lacking for the teams formed to carry out restructuring in the Schools of Tomorrow project. The teams complained most about the shortage of time for individual work and for collaborative work devoted to restructuring activities. When studied by the researchers, almost every team mentioned the problem of time conflicts: difficulty in scheduling meetings and consultations, and problems in managing both their ongoing responsibilities and their new team duties and in simply not having enough time to meet. Sometimes, teams were so overwhelmed that for extended periods they pretty much stopped holding meetings. They found time either by organizing subcommittees or by stealing time from their personal lives (Lieberman et al., 1991).

More time must be made available, if for no other reason than to give teachers a greater opportunity to learn how to perform the new tasks expected of them. "Substantial staff development time must be provided for participating faculties, at least part of this time during the regular school day," says Levine (1991, p. 390) in identifying what is needed for school improvement to succeed. And Shanker (1990) says that staff development should be ongoing and continuous, not consisting simply of workshops held at the school at 3:00. In conjunction with the wholesale upheaval of educational practices in Kentucky, the state school board asked the legislature to allow school systems to convert five instructional days into teacher training days. This request followed the complaints of teachers that they were not adequately prepared to implement the programs in the new educational reform law.

Time in schools is a precious commodity, like water in the desert, that must be conserved and carefully dispensed. When teachers in Iowa were surveyed about changes in their buildings that would be most likely to support reforms, the time-related recommendations included the following:

- Time for team planning, team teaching, and cooperative educa-
  tion. . . .
- Time to plan for comprehensive school transformation through partici-
  patory decision making. . . .
- Time to learn and deploy new technology which improves teaching and
  productivity for students and teachers. . . .
- Redesign of instructional time to include a wider variety of teaching
  strategies. . . .
- A longer teacher contract year. . . .
- Time to participate in state-level professional activities. . . .
- Redesign of the school year—in terms of total hours, not days. . . .
- Relief from distracting intrusions into instructional time. . . .
- Professional discretion over the use of professional time. . . .
- Creation of a maximum class size in traditional instructional class-
  rooms. . . . (Iowa State Education Association, p. 3)

Teachers around the country who are most actively pursuing change often devote large amounts of unpaid work to the effort. This is not to say that teachers should be compensated for every minute spent on the job beyond contracted hours. It does mean, though, that not only must schools be restructured but that the teacher's schedule must be realigned as well. To talk of school restructuring without addressing the problem of time is to imagine that work gets done without anyone doing it. There is an analogy here to the problems that teachers encounter in trying to get all the funding they need to carry out their classroom duties. When time is not built into their schedules for meetings and other team activities, teachers often donate personal time. And when enough money is not available for supplies and programs for students, teachers frequently reach into their own pockets. By their own estimate, more than 40% of the nation's teachers spend at least $400 a year of their own money for supplies and other items related to their teaching (Carnegie Foundation for the Advancement of Teaching, 1990).

A school that is serious about change and about teams of teachers exerting influence beyond the walls of their own classrooms must devise ways to redistribute the work loads of teachers. Reallocated time begins with acceptance of the idea that teachers can be doing their job even when they are not in the presence of students. Recognition of this fact may require a mental readjustment by parents, principals, school administrators, school board members, legislators, and taxpayers. They must reconcile themselves to the idea that when schools are restructured to promote teacher professionalism and teacher inquiry, the time that individual teachers devote to the direct instruction of children will inevitably be reduced (Gideonse, 1990). Change in education will be held back as long as the notion persists that teachers are at work only when they are in their classrooms instructing children.

Many people who are not willing to define teachers' work more broadly can nonetheless appreciate that musicians are working when they are in their living rooms practicing their instruments, that college professors are working when they are in the stacks of the library doing research, that physicians are working when they are attending continuing education courses, or that engineers are working when they are talking over lunch about a project.

One of the most forward-looking approaches to changing the situation for teachers was proposed for the Wells-Ogunquit Community School District in southern Maine, where by the year 2000 there is to be a 50/50 schedule for teachers. The local school committee in 1991 approved an arrangement by which the district's 120 teachers may be able to spend at least half their working time away from their usual instructional duties. This will not necessarily mean being away from students, because an activity such as informally counseling children would be included in the 50% of time free from direct instruction. However, the plan will also open the door further to more time for research, writing, curriculum development, and conferring with colleagues and with student teachers. The school system recognizes that it will probably have to make available more interns and volunteers and engage in differentiated staffing to achieve its 50/50 goal.

Moving in the direction that Wells-Ogunquit envisions would make American schoolteachers more like their counterparts in Japan, who typically spend only about 60% of their school time in the usual classroom activities. They rarely teach more than three hours a day (Cushman, 1992). Japanese teachers have a strong commitment to professionalism and can be found participating in formal research groups, writing journal articles, and taking part in voluntary study groups. However, the schools in Japan are open for classes every day except Sunday, and teachers report to the school on at least half of their 50 to 60 vacation days as well (Sato & McLaughlin, 1992).

Although it is imperative to free teachers intermittently from instructional duties, it is equally essential that this be done in a manner that is minimally disruptive to the continuity of the education of students. This is, after all, an era in which many observers are worried about whether American students are spending sufficient hours in school and are concerned that students do not have enough instructional time. There will be little sympathy for measures that seem to lessen the total time that students devote to meaningful learning. Thus, any attempt to reallocate the time in a teacher's workday must take cognizance of the impact on students. Children, especially in the early grades, may feel abandoned when their teachers suddenly disappear from the classroom during the school day. This apparent dilemma will have to be reconciled sensitively as teachers' schedules are reconfigured.

An extreme response to the need for instructional continuity is virtually never to allow the teacher to be away from the classroom. This is the way many—if not most—schools now operate. At the other extreme, a school might ignore continuity and expose children to a steady flow of substitute teachers, not even trying to get the same sub each time. There is, however, a middle ground that permits teachers to be freed more often from instructional duties without making children feel that they have been deserted. Whatever approach is taken, the aim ought to be to give teachers more time to think, plan, read, confer, learn, and engage in any other activities that promote personal and schoolwide change and improvement. An essential part of this process involves teachers interacting with one another in professional ways. Teachers should have the opportunity for individual growth as well as the chance to work with colleagues, possibly in teams.

A goal in reallocating time should be to make it possible for teachers to do what is necessary to bring deep, lasting change to their schools. This is more than a matter of merely squeezing out additional time for preparation. Too much is at stake to settle for so modest an outcome. In one school in Michigan, teachers at first—not knowing what else to do—used reallocated time only for additional preparation for class. That was not the purpose. "We wanted to get teachers to talk about larger issues, to talk about real study of practice, collaboration, other resources available to them," said the principal. "That requires a different kind of mind-set."

However, as far as preparation time is concerned, it, too, can be adapted to teaming. When preparation time is provided, it is stipulated in a collective bargaining contract that each teacher be allocated a certain number of minutes per day for this purpose. It might be possible for some of this time to be used by team members for joint preparation, working together but still preserving the intent of the provision. More thought should be given to facilitating such collaborative activities. Such an approach would be especially valuable to teachers who are team teaching or working together on interdisciplinary projects. Thus, the team goals and the objectives of the contract may be made to overlap.

SOME WAYS TO REALLOCATE TIME

Whether a teacher works in an elementary school or a secondary school has a bearing on strategies for reallocating time. It is more difficult to find time for a teacher in an elementary school—assigned to a single class for an entire day—to engage in activities not directly related to instruction. Levin (1991) urges that there be recognition of the need of elementary school staff for more of the kind of flexibility in their schedules that those who work in secondary schools customarily have. The schedule of a teacher in a secondary school usually lends itself more readily to adjustments. In high school, for instance, it would be theoretically possible to free up periods by scheduling class meetings three or four times a week, instead of daily. This, after all, is the pattern at colleges. The following are some of the main ways of making more time available for teams of teachers:

> Early dismissal/Late arrival
> Extended lunch
> Longer day/Longer year
> Substitute teachers/Specialist teachers
> Shared students
> New schedules
> Voluntary time
> Other adults in the classroom

Early Dismissal/Late Arrival

Who says that students must always be in the building when teachers are there? What about setting aside some time when only the faculty is in the building, giving them more freedom to engage in team activities and other pursuits that promote professionalism! One way that teachers can gain this sort of time without juggling the schedule and worrying about who is going to cover which class is simply by having the children arrive at school later than the teachers or leave school earlier than the teachers. Some school systems have found this approach quite manageable.

No one seems quite certain when Newton began the practice of early dismissals, but it has been a staple in that suburban Boston district since at least World War I. Children are dismissed early—at 1 P.M.—every Tuesday and Thursday in all 15 elementary schools in the Newton district. Thus, two afternoons a week are available to teachers for pursuing a host of activities, including those that are team related. This gives teachers in the elementary schools four hours a week without students. Newton ends up with fewer instructional hours than most of its neighboring districts, although it still offers enough hours to meet the state minimum requirement.

The time on Tuesday afternoons is generally used for activities in the school building. For example, once or twice a month the principal convenes a faculty meeting on a Tuesday afternoon. Other Tuesday afternoons are used for grade-level, study group, or team meetings; planning sessions; and sometimes conferences with parents. On Thursdays, the time is usually given over to districtwide matters that frequently involve leaving the building. These might be districtwide grade-level meetings, workshops for teachers from various elementary schools who are coordinating subjects in their schools, or districtwide professional development sessions. Teachers remain in their own schools on the Thursdays on which no districtwide functions are scheduled.

In giving its elementary school teachers this kind of schedule, Newton is tacitly telling them that the district understands that they need time away from students if they are going to be able to interact with one another. "It reinforces for teachers that we support the concept of working together," said David C. Michaud, associate superintendent for elementary education in Newton.

An approach of this sort is used in some other districts as well. In 1972, teachers in Fairfax County, Virginia, agreed in negotiations to add a half hour to the elementary school day from Tuesday through Friday if, in return, students would be dismissed two and a half hours early each Monday so that extra time could be made available for teachers to work without students.

An important feature of the Fairfax schedule was not merely that it provided extra hours each week for teachers in elementary schools to have time for possible team activities, but that the time was available in blocks allowing for sustained effort. It isn't simply that teachers need time when they don't have to worry about students—there are 150 minutes a week of individual preparation time in Fairfax elementary schools—but that there be enough of it in chunks that permit extended interaction during periods when colleagues are available. In Fairfax, for instance, elementary school teachers who work together in an interdisciplinary language arts program need time on a regular basis for collaborative planning.

However, after almost 20 years of following this schedule, a move was made to revise the arrangement so that teachers in Fairfax would spend the time with students instead of being away from them. Changing the schedule in this way would add the equivalent of almost three weeks to the school year for students. Sympathy for such a change reflected national concern about declining achievement in American schools, which some observers attribute to the fact that the United States has a shorter school year than many other countries. Teachers in Fairfax objected, however, and fought successfully to retain the early dismissal. It was an unfortunate battle in which each side espoused a reasonable position.

Extended Lunch

The lunch period for teachers is extended to twice its normal length every other Friday at Kendon Elementary School in Lansing, Michigan. This means that for 80 minutes, the teachers are able to have the kind of concentrated, duty-free time together that those who work in elementary schools seldom get. Typically, a portion of the time is given over to a whole-faculty activity and the other half to meeting in teams or small groups. This opportunity comes on top of the half day a week that is available to teachers for meetings of study groups.

Meanwhile, the school's 300 students—except the kindergarteners, whose school day ends at the start of lunch—spend the time eating, playing at recess, and attending an activity with educational content. The educational activity is held twice during the teachers' extended lunch so that half of the students can be at recess while the rest attend the activity. Thus, one particular Friday in January, students gathered for a film on the Reverend Martin Luther King, Jr., whose birthday fell that month. Aides are hired specifically to come to the school during the extended lunch to be with the children. Having the students eat in their classrooms with the aides helps minimize rowdiness.

For all its advantages, the extended lunch is not a panacea for the time problem. The period can easily degenerate into a long babysitting session if students are not productively engaged. Kendon tried to counter this possibility by expecting teachers to use the occasion of, say, the King film to do some teaching in advance that would present questions and ideas for children to keep in mind as they watched the film. Then, afterward, children could discuss the movie with these questions and ideas in mind. There is the issue, though, of whether enough quality programs can be presented to students on a regular basis to keep the extended lunch worthwhile for them while their teachers are benefiting from the time away from the classroom ("Making Time," 1990).

Longer Day/Longer Year

Much of the discussion about adding to the time that American children spend in school—as illustrated in Fairfax County—revolves around the fact that students in the United States spend fewer hours and fewer days in school than their counterparts in some Asian and European countries. By the time they have completed the sixth grade, for example, students in Japan and China have spent the equivalent of one to two years longer in school than Americans (Stevenson & Stigler, 1992). Although American children spend an average of 180 days a year in school, the school year is, for example, 243 days in Japan, 220 days in Korea, 216 days in Luxembourg, 200 days in the Netherlands, and 195 days in Hong Kong (Barrett, 1990). International comparisons of student achievement that reveal a low rank for Americans reinforce arguments for lengthening the amount of time that students spend in school. The Labor and Human Resources Committee of the U.S. Senate even provided $1 million in 1991 to set up the National Education Commission on Time and Learning to study the idea of lengthening the school day and the school year.

A chief impetus for school improvement in recent years has been a concern about America's ability to remain economically competitive. There is merit to this argument, but it usually seems to take no account of the hundreds of thousands of menial jobs that are lost to other parts of the world not because workers elsewhere are smarter but because they work for less money. Also seldom mentioned in discussions about a longer school day and a longer school year is the fact that teachers in Japan and China are typically given a substantial portion of the school day for planning and other duties without having to be in charge of a class ("Asians Far Outstrip," 1991; Stigler & Stevenson, 1991).

Yet, more is at stake in lengthening the school year or the school day than instructional time for students. Seldom in the debate is mention made of teachers, except to note that asking them to work more hours during the year will inevitably mean having to raise their salaries. More immediately related to the concerns of this book is the idea that an extended calendar could open all sorts of possibilities for new scheduling arrangements for teachers. More time might be found during a longer employment contract for teachers to be able to give greater attention to activities in which they engage with colleagues for the purpose of becoming better teachers. As it is, regulations in most states already designate a certain number of days each school year as time for staff development. If the school day and/or the school year were lengthened primarily for the benefit of students, there would be much greater latitude for professional activities as well.

A main target of the campaign to lengthen the school year is summer vacation, a respite of almost three months during which some students—especially those who already lag—tend to divorce themselves from the habits of book learning. In the fall, it takes weeks, if not months, to reintroduce them to the printed word and get them back to the point they had reached when school was dismissed in June (Heyns, 1978). Some may think that year-round schooling is the answer, but in almost all places in the country where schools are open on a 12-month basis, the school year has not been lengthened for individual students. The buildings are used throughout the year, but the number of vacation days for students tends to remain the same as in the traditional schedule. It's just that the breaks are spread over 12 months instead of being concentrated in the summer months and that students attend school on staggered schedules. These are basically schemes for better utilizing school facilities, not for adding to instructional time.

For all the talk about longer school days and longer school years, not much has happened. The length of the school year in almost all states remains about 180 days (Education Commission of the States, 1989). Some commentators maintain that despite the focus on the length of the school year and student achievement, Americans believe deep down that the existing schedule is a reasonable one. It may very well be that the nation is complacent about lengthening the school year because it doesn't want to complicate life for families who plan on a school-free summer (Barrett, 1990).

Whatever enthusiasm might be generated for adding to the school day or the school year, a formidable barrier remains to be overcome. Teachers are certain to object to any scheme that calls for them to add to their working hours without extra pay. In 1992, when the Washington, D.C., public schools proposed to add 15 minutes of class time to the beginning and end of each school year, the plan was generally hailed by parents and condemned by teachers, who charged that they had not been consulted. The extra instructional time in this case did not mean that teachers were to spend 30 more minutes in the building, but that they would have to give up half of the preparation time that had been available before and after classes.

Longer school days and longer school years will not materialize in American public schools without some struggles. The decade of the 1990s has ushered in an era of tight budgets, and one has to wonder how readily more money would be made available for schools to pay teachers who might end up not spending the entire additional time with students. A compelling case will have to be made for the idea that in the long run, students might be better off if their teachers had a little more time when they were not with students.

Substitute Teachers/Specialist Teachers

The Rockefeller Foundation and other sponsors of team building have tried to help the process by allocating money for hiring substitute teachers to fill in for regular teachers when they are absent for team activities during the school day. This is an obvious concession to the fact that team building, properly pursued, inevitably requires teachers sometimes to be away from their students during the hours when classes are in session. But for a whole host of reasons known to anyone who has ever been a student in a classroom staffed by a substitute, this is not the ideal solution to finding time during the school day for teams to meet.

When Holmes Middle School in Flint, Michigan, first reallocated time for all of the teachers in one wing of the building so that they could have half a day together each week throughout a semester, the school sent substitutes into their classrooms each Thursday morning. The teachers welcomed the freedom and what it meant for their ability to move toward change, but they found themselves returning to their classrooms with a sense of dread. The substitutes were little more than strangers walking through an unfamiliar neighborhood, and the students acted out every mischievous and aggressive fantasy they ever harbored. The regular teachers were not sure it was worth it.

The candid appraisal of someone who was a substitute at the school during this period attested to the difficulties: "You struggle with how to make that time meaningful for the children in the classroom. Do you teach what the teacher suggests or do you teach something totally different? How do you come to agreement with the teacher about what's going to happen during that time?"

Finally, in recognition of such problems, a new approach was tried the next year. Three so-called resource teachers were hired as, in effect, regular substitutes for teachers who received reallocated time. No longer would as many teachers be released at once, but those who were away from their classrooms did not have to pay for their absence with a guilty conscience. The same resource teacher showed up in the same classroom each week at the same time; she got to know the students and the students got to know her. Furthermore, there was ongoing contact between the resource teacher and the regular teacher to try to make the instructional transition as smooth as possible.

This approach is a response to the concern of teachers around the country who wonder whether it is wise to get instruction-free time if it means leaving their students in the hands of the sort of substitutes ordinarily used in schools. The following are some of the questions that ought to guide any program that involves having someone fill in for the regular teacher:

> How many different adult faces will the students have to see when their regular teacher is not available to them? In other words, will the same person or a different person fill in each time?
> How different will the replacement's style be from that of the regular teacher?
> How much continuity will there be between the lesson taught by the substitute and what is taught by the regular teacher?
> How extensively will the regular teacher confer with the person who fills in?

A resource teacher hired at Holmes told me that she considered the plan successful. "The students get familiar with you," she said. "They are more able to relate to you, more able to respect you. Otherwise, with the usual sub, there is a tendency for them to give her a hard time. I stay with the lesson plan of the teacher. The teacher normally arrives back in the room just before the end of the class and we confer." She added that she thought another benefit of the plan to the students was that it "gives the students a break from the regular teacher."

Another of the resource teachers had the advantage of having previously worked as a student teacher in the wing of the school in which she was now filling in for the regular teacher. The setting and the students were familiar to her, and she was unfazed by the misconduct she encountered. "The kids who act up for me are the ones who act up for the regular teacher," she said knowingly. "The kids consider me as one of their regular teachers, not as a sub. As a result, I enjoy it."

As for the regular teachers, they thought that in the best of all worlds, they would never leave their students during the school day. But they wanted to believe that in the long run their students would be better off if the teachers were away for periods of time because the instructional program would be improved by what the teachers would be able to do as a result of those absences. One of the teachers had this to say about having a resource teacher available to replace her: "This way, the sub is the same each time and the kids know her. I usually give her something to do with them. The more she works with me, the more I get to know her. I don't think it's the perfect answer, but it's better than last year."

A variation on this approach is the schedule in some elementary and middle schools that calls for students to meet with specialist teachers in such subjects as art, music, and physical education during the time that regular teachers gather with teammates. Or in some schools, students might be scheduled to be in the library or the computer room during this period. Thus, rather than use substitutes—even ones who fill in on a regular basis as the resource teachers do at Holmes—a school might allocate time for regular classroom teachers to be free by scheduling ancillary subjects during these periods.

Shared Students

Implicit in the team approach as described in this book is the idea of members of a team having time together without students. A team cannot fully function without the availability of such time for discussing and planning. Middle schools have perhaps gone furthest toward fulfilling this vision. At Eggers Middle School in Hammond, Indiana, for instance, the classic block schedule is used. For teachers, this means daily back-to-back periods—a total of 90 minutes—during which a team of about 10 members can meet. The faculty is divided into three such teams with about 270 children in each of the learning communities for which a team is responsible.

The first of the two successive 45-minute segments is typically designated as community planning time. It is a period during which the team discusses such matters as interdisciplinary teaching, thematic units, and individual students. This time also might be used for conferences with students or parents or with representatives of social service agencies. Usually, the second 45 minutes is devoted to individual planning. There is, however, flexibility that allows the team to divide up the 90 minutes each day as it sees fit.

Where are the children during the hour and a half that they are not with the teachers in their learning community? Again, Eggers follows what has become accepted practice in the middle schools that use block scheduling and provide time for teams of teachers to meet. The students spend this time in such ancillary courses as music, art, home economics, industrial arts, computer literacy, and physical education. This is what makes it possible to free the teachers who are teaching the main academic subjects in the interdisciplinary team program. Students in some middle schools go to the ancillary courses only two or three times a week, and so the teacher teams meet only two or three times a week. Eggers is different from those schools in that students are sent to the ancillary courses each day, which allows daily team gatherings.

Yet, not all middle schools or all teams that share students can look forward to such salutary scheduling. A study in 1989 found that only about one third of middle schools that use teams provided teachers with two or more hours of common planning time during the course of a week (Lewis, 1992).

New Schedules

Adjustments to the schedule can have mutual benefit to students and teachers. This is particularly true at the secondary school level, where the 45-minute class can be a constraint on learning. Students go to five, six, or even seven of these classes each day. It is taken for granted that they are supposed to juggle five, six, or seven subjects at once during the academic term and that the courses are to be carved into brief time segments that require students to spend the day switching their minds on and off, like light bulbs, as they proceed from one discipline to another. There is more emphasis on covering each subject than on learning it. In spite of the logic of abandoning this approach, few schools have attempted to make fundamental changes in the way courses are scheduled (Miller, 1992).

In the name of better learning, however, a different kind of schedule should be used, particularly in secondary schools. As changes are made in the ways that schedules are drawn, it should be done so as to minimize conflicts and maximize opportunities for students (Tewel, 1991a). A by-product of such restructuring might be that teachers, too, would gain schedules that are more amenable to their professionalism and to the collaborative work of teams. Once basic adjustments are made in the schedule to promote the interests of students, questions could be posed about other constraints that are built into schedules as they are now constructed. Advocates of the Coalition of Essential Schools, the Paideia Program, and other programs are challenging the existing schedules for secondary education.

The coalition, for instance, strives to simplify the secondary school schedule and provide students with sustained periods of time in which to concentrate on their work without having to get up and go to another class. Among the practices used are the elimination of electives by folding them into interdisciplinary courses; the scheduling of special courses that may be taken by a small number of students—say, calculus or chorus—before or after the sustained interdisciplinary blocks so as not to be disruptive; and the use of back-to-back courses at the same grade level so that teachers have the option of running a period longer, if necessary (Coalition of Essential Schools, 1989).

The main way of changing the schedule is to have students take fewer courses at any one time and to build longer periods and more flexibility into the daily schedule so that the idea that knowledge has to be dispensed in 45-minute segments is dealt a death blow. One such innovation has been the Copernican Plan developed by Joseph M. Carroll, the superintendent of the Masconomet Regional School District in Topsfield, Massachusetts. Alternative schedules are used in the Copernican Plan. Students take either one four-hour class each school day for

30 days or two two-hour classes for 60 days. Either way, the full day would also have time for seminars, study help, physical education, music, activities, and lunch.

The teacher as well as the student does less mental juggling under this plan. The teacher has fewer separate preparations and a more intensive period in which to get to know the student. Carroll told me that he believes the Copernican Plan would work best if teachers operated in teams and if there were opportunities for the team members to interact during the day. In most instances in which the plan has been used so far, however, it has not been with an eye toward opening up this kind of time for teacher teams.

Voluntary Time

One way in which those who work in schools have most frequently found time for collaboration is by voluntarily making it available. A reason why teachers have so often had to donate their time is because it is so unusual for time to be built into the schedule for teachers to work together. As it turns out, voluntary meetings of this sort are held before school starts in the morning, during lunchtime, in the afternoon after the formal school day has ended, on weekday evenings, and on weekends at one or another's homes. Attendance is not required, and there is no remuneration.

Some groups of teachers who work together even schedule such voluntary meetings on a regular basis. I have come across teams that meet, for instance, every Tuesday morning at 7:00 or every Thursday afternoon at 3:30. A principal who was the member of one such team said, "The six of us meet from 6:30 to 8:00 one morning a week. It is the only way that we can find time for the team. You'll do that for a while, but at some point you say, 'No more.'"

Members of one team told me that they met at each other's homes every other Saturday morning, a time when they certainly would not be expected to be conferring with colleagues. This is the only way that some teams find that they are able to function. School schedules have not been sufficiently reconfigured to accommodate the needs of teams, and little money has been allocated to pay people for their extra time.

Teams meet on their own time because they need to get the work of the team accomplished. It is also a way that they can demonstrate their dedication. Furthermore, it is not altogether unreasonable to expect committed people to give some of their own time to a worthwhile pursuit. It happens all the time in any number of fields, and it certainly occurs in connection with charitable and service activities.

Yet, it is troubling when virtually the only way teams can meet is as a result of their willingness to sacrifice their own time. When work schedules make inadequate allowance for team gatherings, surely those schedules are shortsighted. Schools can show support for teamwork by making it more possible for members to meet during the regular workday, when they are paid for their dedication. As the member of one team said:

> If you want people to attend meetings, to do research, or whatever, you have to provide time and can't always expect teachers to go to meetings from 3:30 to 6:00 or during a dinner at night. You're tired from having taught all day and have to do it all again the next day. There have to be resources of some kind to free teachers.

Other Adults in the Classroom

Finally, time can sometimes be made available for teams by regarding the work with students as a shared responsibility. Teacher's aides, student teachers, and parent and community volunteers might all spend time with students, making it possible for teachers occasionally to attend to noninstructional tasks alone or with colleagues. As matters now stand, the presence of others in the classroom is not so much used as an opportunity to let the teacher leave the room as to supplement the teacher. Usually, when there is an extra adult in the classroom, it becomes an occasion for more small-group and individual instruction.

However, the availability of another adult might also be used as a chance for the regular teacher to attend to teamwork, if only to confer quietly in a corner with a team member who comes to the room while her own class is with the gym teacher or art teacher.

It is not likely that enough use will be made of other adults to free great amounts of time for teamwork, but some small contributions can be made this way. There are times, too, when other adults might actually take over the class for a more extended period, giving the teacher an even greater opportunity for noninstructional work. Teachers at the Louis Pasteur School in Chicago, for example, were able to gather once a month while students were on day-long field trips or half-day assemblies funded by a grant from the Joyce Foundation. Parents were recruited to oversee the children during these activities ("Carving Out Time," 1991).

—— 9

Obstacles to teams ——

Every attempt by a team of teachers to improve a school is a tale of struggles to overcome obstacles. Schools are not institutions waiting passively to be changed. Each school is a social organism with its own customs and traditions, a unique history, and sets of distinct behavioral expectations for each group whose lives it touches: the teachers, the administrators, the students, and the parents. Any attempt by a team to disrupt these patterns is no less cataclysmic than trying to alter the patterns of a family or a neighborhood.

Furthermore, pressures from outside the school may make the work of teams, however highly dedicated, exceedingly problematic. Even if all the internal difficulties attendant to team building are conquered, teams may fail because of impediments that originate outside the school. A school that is successful in creating a wonderful climate for learning in the building, for instance, can find it impossible to overcome the vicissitudes of forces beyond the school's walls. The violence, drugs, and family disintegration of the larger society may still overwhelm children who return home each day to circumstances that may not be friendly to education. Thus, successful outcomes for teams may depend as much on surmounting these external barriers as they do on such factors as selecting the team, training the team, and winning the support of colleagues.

Some obstacles to teams are predictable, which makes them no less formidable, and others—like a state trooper operating a radar trap around the next turn—can appear suddenly and unexpectedly. Leadership in this kind of endeavor in part means being sufficiently prepared and committed to confront and deal with challenges that come out of nowhere. The impending difficulties that a school team face should not be a signal to leave the status quo undisturbed but should instead serve as reminders that the process of school improvement will be wrenching and perhaps even unsuccessful. It is only reasonable to proceed with an understanding of the obstacles and a willingness to suffer recurring setbacks. Like Jehovah's Witnesses, who get used to having doors slammed in their faces, team members who accept the burden of leading change in their schools must be ready for rebuffs.

Because so little has changed in the ways that schools operate despite the periodic reform movements, it follows that teams will not necessarily be greeted with hosannas. Consider the reform movement that began in 1983, for example. Its impact has been, at best, indirect on the manner in which teachers teach and students learn. Almost any adult of any age anywhere in this country could wander into a classroom and find that what is occurring is roughly equivalent to what that adult encountered one, two, or even three generations ago. "I've taught public school for 26 years but I just can't do it anymore," said John Taylor Gatto (1991), a New York State Teacher of the Year, complaining about what he considered the many stultifying practices in schools. "Reforms come and go—without changing much. Even reformers can't imagine school much different" (p. A8).

In tracing the course of team building, I have tried throughout this book to give a sense of the barriers involved, step by step. The previous chapter was devoted to one of the most persistent of those barriers: time. In light of such obstacles, team building alone is no guarantee of school improvement, although it is spreading and winning adherents. Some sponsors have done more than others to try to overcome the obstructions. In Minnesota, this effort has involved pinpointing the critical variables considered crucial to the team's long-term success. To the extent that these variables are present in a school, the school is deemed by officials in Minnesota to have a greater chance for implementing a successful school improvement program. The following are some of those variables (Minnesota Department of Education, 1991):

1. A plan for school improvement that is known, shared, and supported by the leadership team, the building staff, the district administration and the school board. . . .
2. The district administration and the school board consistently allocate resources (time and money) to support school improvement efforts beyond a school's first year of involvement. . . .
3. In-school time is available for leadership team planning. . . .
4. Leadership teams feel they have access to and receive support from designated support systems, in particular the regional facilitator. . . .
5. The principal plays a major role in the successful implementation of a improvement program. . . .
6. Being a member of the leadership team is a positive experience. . . .
7. Leadership team members feel they have the knowledge and skills to develop and implement a school improvement program. . . .

8. Contract negotiation disputes influence progress toward school improvement. (pp. 8–9)

Variables much like those listed in Minnesota affect the work of teams in schools everywhere. Conditions in several key areas exert an enormous influence on the variables, posing potential obstacles, and go a long way toward determining whether teams will succeed or fail. The following are the main areas in which teams most often confront barriers:

Societal factors
Budgets
Unions
Teacher knowledge and dedication
Team function
Continuity

SOCIETAL FACTORS

Members of teams are not miracle workers. In some schools, especially in urban districts, the societal problems are of such magnitude that even the most conscientious work by teams may barely make a difference. In these settings, getting through the day, not team building, is paramount. Students suffer under a scourge of drugs, poverty, and crime. Families scarcely exist for some of these young people, and pregnancy prematurely ends the education of large numbers of females. Schools become places where teachers and students worry constantly about safely traveling back and forth and about being able to avoid physical harm in the building.

One of every three boys in America's high schools carries a gun, a knife, or some other weapon to school at least once a month because, these youngsters say, the weapon may be needed for protection ("20% in High Schools," 1991). In Los Angeles, the shooting on nearby streets got so bad that students in school rooms were taught to stay away from windows and to slither along the floor rather than pass by some windows (Mydans, 1991). Education came to a virtual halt at Centennial High School in Compton, California, as a result of gang activity; there was no chance for any learning to occur in the school until authorities recaptured control of the building by some tough-minded actions (Putka, 1991).

Team building can easily be perceived as a frivolity in schools where education is reduced to a survival exercise. How can teachers come to behave more professionally when everything around them seems to render their efforts futile? This is not to say that teams have no relevance to the most troubled schools, but clearly in such settings, teams must struggle mightily.

Even in the absence of the most egregious outside obstacles, a multitude of other societal pressures continue to impinge on schools in most neighborhoods, suburban as well as urban. Students of varying socioeconomic backgrounds denigrate the values represented by education and shun the hard work that often underpins success in school. They reserve their best efforts for part-time jobs that many of them do not need except in the pursuit of greater material acquisition. Sports and entertainment—are they really any different?—exert tremendous influence on the young, which complicates enormously the job of teachers. Can team building make any more difference in improving teaching and learning than have a host of other innovations that have been thwarted by barriers of this sort?

BUDGETS

There is no escaping the fact that it costs money to improve schools. A Leadership Academy such as the one sponsored by Rockefeller could cost perhaps $5,000 for each participant in a four-week residential program. There are other, less expensive ways of carrying out team building, but however it is done, there will almost certainly be an extra expense for building teams. This is a sad reality at a time when education is under severe financial restraints. The pressures are sobering when one considers how little extra money schools have available.

When the 1991–1992 school year opened, some 15,000 experienced teachers across the country were told that they could not return to their jobs because those positions had been eliminated to save money. In Minnesota, the state's Teacher of the Year was laid off for the fourth time in her 13-year career. Chicago asked its teachers to forgo a 7% raise they were scheduled to receive. Altogether, more than 30 states faced budget deficits, and cutbacks loomed in state allotments for local schools. An indication that the fiscal situation has grown more dire is the finding of the National Education Association (NEA) that labor strikes by teachers increased by 36% in the fall of 1991 (Diegmueller, 1991).

Overwhelmed school systems remain desperate for funds. Central Falls School District in Rhode Island asked the state to take it over because it did not have the wherewithal to continue. Richmond Unified School District in California closed down for a period because it ran out of money. In New York City, the nation's largest school system looked at the prospect of losing $465 million from its $7 billion budget. Art and music classes were cut, the corps of counselors had to be reduced, ragged textbooks had to make it through another year, and a model program that provided mentors for inexperienced teachers became nothing more than a luxury to be discarded.

For years, the parents of America's schoolchildren said that the biggest problem that education faced was poor discipline and, in more recent years, drugs. In 1991, however, the Gallup poll found that parents of schoolchildren considered a lack of adequate financial support the main problem that the nation's public schools confront. It is entirely understandable that under such circumstances, prospects are not favorable for innovative professional development programs for teachers. But policymakers must come to realize that all of the talk about school reform will be idle chatter if teachers are not equipped to implement the changes. Schools do not change themselves. There is no deus ex machina to intervene in this drama. Teachers themselves will have to make change happen in schools. Otherwise, America's schools will be about the same at the end of the decade as they were at the beginning.

It will obviously curtail the prospects for team building if funds are not allocated for this purpose. Money is needed to train teams and to enable them to do their work, if only to hire enough additional staff to free team members for the work they are to do. Insufficient resources was perhaps the most important limitation on teams that operated in New York City public schools through the Schools of Tomorrow project (Lieberman et al., 1991).

Much of the progress so far in team building within schools has been made possible by an infusion of extra money from foundations and other sponsors, but these outside sources cannot be counted on in the long run. Ultimately, if team building is to figure prominently in the national effort to improve elementary and secondary education, regular school revenues will have to be involved. One approach might be to pay team members stipends for attending an academy and to reward them with bonuses for the work they do in the school on behalf of the team. Teachers' contracts could designate such activities as a basic part of employment for those who get involved.

Given the fiscal pressures on elementary and secondary education today, it is more likely that the idea of encouraging voluntary, unpaid work by teams is apt to have a certain appeal. This might be acceptable under some circumstances in some school systems, but the ramifications of such a policy would have to be weighed on a highly sensitive scale. Therefore, the question about team building is whether it will be able to attract enough sustenance to survive and prosper in the nation's school districts.

UNIONS

Some of the most enlightened support for teacher-led school change has come from the mouths of the national presidents of the two major teacher organizations: Albert Shanker of the American Federation of Teachers (AFT) and Mary Futrell and her successor, Keith Geiger, of the NEA. They and those closest to them have been personally responsible for some of the major breakthroughs in persuading members of local chapters to dare to be courageous on behalf of school improvement. Leaders in local unions such as those of the AFT at Pittsburgh, Toledo, and Rochester and those of the NEA at Jefferson County, Kentucky, Bellevue, Washington, and Greece, New York, have displayed the same sort of convictions as their national leaders.

Yet, by and large, achievements of this sort at the local level by units of both the NEA and the AFT are anomalies. Union leadership in too many school systems stands in the way of improvement—not because leaders of local bargaining units do not want students to have richer educational experiences but because they worry about the implications for teachers. They fear that jobs may be lost, work may be made more difficult and more demanding, new knowledge may be required, and personal inadequacies may be exposed. Change is threatening to teachers, just as it is to assembly-line workers at General Motors or to dentists who have not learned the latest techniques in cosmetic dentistry. For unions to fulfill their democratic potential, however, they must go beyond simply looking out for teachers and demand that schools be structured so as to sustain teachers in cultivating the capacity for critical deliberation in their classrooms (Gutmann, 1987).

Issues surrounding team building that can lead to disputes with unions range from determining which schools should be involved to who should be on the teams and to the roles that the teams should play in their schools. Unions will have to be flexible for team building to flourish and for teams to be able to pursue their work effectively. Teams are not likely to operate successfully where heavy constraints are imposed by a union local—or by the central administration, for that matter. Team building is impaired if collective bargaining contracts are unyielding in their requirements.

On the other hand, this is a time when America is pervaded by criticism of collective bargaining and unions are regarded as ugly, oppressive, goonish, primitive, undignified, and a threat to individual liberty

(Geoghegan, 1992). Commentators must be wary of blaming unions instinctively for the failures of team building. There is a great deal that can go wrong with team building that may at first glance appear to be related to the bargaining contract or to union foot-dragging when actually there may be other culprits.

In this pilot stage of team building, although intransigence always looms as a possible obstacle, unions have tended not to be negative players in the game of team building. There is reason for optimism. As Shedd and Bachrach (1991) point out, the strength of any union depends as much on its ability to accommodate management's interests as on its ability to threaten. If management demonstrates that it is willing to support team building for the good of students, then unions, too, ought to be ready to cooperate in this pursuit.

TEACHER KNOWLEDGE AND DEDICATION

Membership on a team can enhance an educator's ability and effectiveness. For the team itself to attain success, though, the members must possess a good deal more than what is usually provided through an academy for team building, which cannot compensate fully for gaps in the knowledge and commitment of teachers and principals. Often, teachers lack the knowledge and skills to examine the processes and structure of the system or to investigate the interrelationships of the parts of that system (Basom & Crandall, 1991). In other words, someone whose work is marginal is not apt to be converted into a paradigm of educational professionalism as a result of being on or being influenced by a team.

Nor is the support of the team apt to be sufficient to fill serious holes in, say, a teacher's subject content knowledge. Amid all the talk of changing curriculums to lend more depth and coherence to subjects, there is not enough discussion of how teachers are expected to be able to teach the new curriculum. In identifying systemic barriers to educational change, Smith and O'Day (1991) make the point that neither their pre-service nor their in-service education has equipped teachers for the job.

A factor that may militate against the work of teams, therefore, is the level of competence of members and potential members. It is fine to be enthusiastic about team building, but the team's ability to make a difference can be limited by the abilities of those who are to be the agents of change. In England, for example, it was found by Her Majesty's Inspectorate and the Department of Education and Science that the greatest obstacle to the continued improvement of students in science "was that many teachers lack a working knowledge of elementary science" (Bennett & Carre, 1991, p. 14). A similar observation could undoubtedly be made in the United States.

Competence cannot be taken for granted. When principals and teachers in the Washington, D.C., public school system were asked what portion of the teaching force in their school was incompetent, they consistently indicated that they felt that between 10% and 20% per school fell into this category (Willrich, 1991). In Washington's districtwide teaching force of some 6,700, that portion would translate into 670 to 1,340 incompetents. The level of incompetence ascribed to teachers in Washington was in line with the national average of 5% to 15% estimated in the *New York Times* (Mansnerus, 1992). Yet, in Washington, as in most school systems, only a handful of teachers are dismissed for reasons of incompetence. Granted, some voluntarily depart the ranks in tacit acknowledgment of their ineptitude, but enough incompetent people are left on the staff to present a large obstacle to school improvement.

Furthermore, any consideration of the barriers to improvement must take note of the many teachers who have no formal preparation for the task to which they are assigned. In secondary schools, for example, 33% of science teachers and 40% of mathematics teachers neither majored in their subject nor were certified to teach it as their primary field of assignment ("Teachers' Majors," 1991). This is not necessarily the fault of the teachers. Many are pressed into service because those with proper credentials are not available. Others, however, accept inappropriate assignments because of contractually provided seniority that allows them to remain employed even though they lack the qualifications. In any event, the upshot is that students are shortchanged.

Team building, if successful, might help improve the work of some of the teachers and principals who, for one reason or another, are performing inadequately or are in positions for which they have not been adequately prepared. But team building is not alchemy, and it probably will not transform someone who does not want to improve or is incapable of doing better.

TEAM FUNCTION

A team is weakened when its role and purpose in the school are unclear. A lack of clarity in its mission can defeat a team as readily as having unsuitable members. Inherent in team building are some contradictions that sometimes make it almost unavoidable that a team's function will pose potential problems. It may be unclear, no matter how thorough the training in the academy, how the team is to go about putting into practice what it has learned.

There is more than one way for a team to be a team, and some of the ways may not be appropriate to the situation in a particular school. Drucker (1992) uses a sports analogy to delineate the roles of at least three different kinds of teams, asserting that a major reason for the failure of teams is the assumption that there is just one way for a team to act. First, he mentions baseball, where players mainly play *on* the team rather than *as* a team. Like workers on an assembly line, they have mostly fixed positions. Second, he cites the football team, which also has mostly fixed positions. However, like the symphony orchestra, they play *as* a team and follow a score or, if you will, a play book. Third is the tennis doubles team on which players have primary rather than fixed positions. This is a team in which players customarily cover for each other, as workers do in a flexible-manufacturing plant, and they must be trained together and work together for a period of time before functioning fully as a team.

In general, academies have not given enough attention to the manner in which the team is supposed to carry out its work in the school. As was noted in chapter 7, personal transformation is not enough to justify team building. There has to be more. Will the team, for instance, be on safe and approved ground if it anoints itself as the consultative body to the principal? Will the rest of the teachers endorse that role? And if a team takes a more specialized form—say, a grade-level team or a subject area team—what will be the relationship of the team to the rest of the faculty who are not involved with that grade level or that subject?

Some teams are not provided with a process for pursuing change. They are equipped with new ideas, but very little is said about the process by which those ideas can be passed along to others and implemented. They end up without knowledge of a change process. Nor, even if they have learned a change process, do they necessarily learn a process by which they can teach the process.

There is confusion, too, about how much of an agenda the team can set for the whole school and how great a role it can reserve for itself in shaping and implementing the agenda. At the beginning, when a team is selected and preparing to go off to the team building experience, it is difficult for the members to indicate precisely what they will bring back because, obviously, they have not yet had the experience of the academy. On the other hand, during team building, when the team is sharpening its vision of the future, it dare not be too specific about its role in the school because that role must be subject to what is acceptable to the rest of the staff.

Finally, a question must be raised about whether the team is the right unit for initiating change in a school. Such a presumption underlies team building. But Druckman and Bjork (1991) maintain that the "long-term training of teams has rarely been studied" and that "the review of what we know about group performance is more striking for what is missing than for what is known" (p. 257). What evidence is there then that working through a team is better than working through the entire faculty? In 1992, Accelerated Schools began shifting away from a team approach and adopted a whole-faculty approach for indoctrination to its philosophy. Henry Levin was not satisfied that training teams and sending them back to train their colleagues was sufficiently effective. "We want a better batting average," he said in an interview. Some of those associated with an attempt to restructure a high school in Arkansas concluded that such an effort should probably begin with a least a third of the faculty and move as quickly as possible to include the entire faculty (Nickle, Flynt, Poynter, & Rees, Jr., 1990).

There is even something slightly unsettling about the idea that members of the school community would be better off in teams than working alone. Granted that teachers who go off for training by themselves have great difficulty after their return in promoting change beyond the confines of their own classrooms. Maybe, however, in the final analysis, it will turn out that the best that can be expected is for classrooms to improve individually rather than collaboratively. Is there sufficient evidence that schools improve when teachers work together?

Judith Warren Little (quoted in Fullan, 1990) asks whether "we have in teachers' collaborative work the creative development of well informed choices, or the mutual reinforcement of poorly informed habit?" (p. 14). Fullan (1990) speaks of "contrived collegiality" that "can ignore the real culture of the school and lead to a proliferation of unwanted contacts among teachers that consume already scarce time with little show for it" (p. 15). Despite the criticism of teacher isolation and the praise for interaction among teachers, perhaps it may turn out that the best for which anyone can hope is a school building full of extremely able individual practitioners who continue in the tradition of having little to do with each other but a whole lot to do with their students.

CONTINUITY

Nothing can detract from a team's effectiveness more quickly than the departure from the school of some of the team's members. A team, like a white corpuscle fighting disease, is a small and fragile cell in a large and sometimes hostile body. If the team shrinks, the remaining members will not only have to enlarge their individual responsibilities but will also be left with fewer involved colleagues to nurture and sustain them.

School faculties are often in flux. This is both an advantage and a disadvantage to the school. The vitality provided by an infusion of new blood contributes to the rejuvenation of the school and helps introduce new ideas and variations of practice. However, the loss of veteran members of the faculty means that professional relationships that have existed for years are suddenly lost. This is doubly troublesome when the person who departs is a member of a team that has been carefully cultivated to bring change to the school.

The size of the team is reduced, and the time and expense that were devoted to making the departing teacher part of the team has been squandered. Members of some teams studied for this book left their schools even before the first year had elapsed. This is not unusual. At an elementary school in Kansas City, Kansas, 8 of 13 teachers left after winning a grant from RJR Nabisco for implementing reforms, although all had signed a statement of support for the grant (Sommerfeld, 1992). The whole idea of creating a team is that the members will operate as a unit, complementing and reinforcing one another. The synergy of the melded whole is to be more powerful than the sum of its individual parts. By the very nature of the team building process, teams are small. But turnover can render this smallness a disadvantage.

Ideally, those who embark on team building will agree to remain at the school for a given number of years after the training. Furthermore, the district administration might promise neither to dismiss members of the team because of layoffs nor to make unrequested reassignments of team members to other schools for a specified period. A promise by a teacher to remain at a school can, of course, only be voluntary. A teacher retains the right to job mobility and ought not be inextricably bound to a school. But one would hope that those sufficiently serious about school change to participate in team building would see the wisdom of voluntarily staying at a school for a reasonable period.

As was pointed out in chapter 6, what is said about the detrimental effect of teacher turnover can be repeated about principals—and even more so. No one's continuity on the team counts for more than the principal's. Usually, it is in the nature of a principal's upward mobility to shift from school to school, taking on gradually more challenging and more lucrative administrative assignments. But a principal who participates in team building should—just as the teachers—be willing to make a commitment to the school for a reasonable period.

As team building is so new in education, not much thought has been given to what must be done to rejuvenate a team. Once the team is established and functioning, it has to be cognizant of not neglecting itself and its own development (Stokes, 1982). For how long does the magic of the academy weave its spell? David Colton, the professor who helped oversee the Leadership Academy operated by the University of

New Mexico, says, "In the summer, you can energize and change a group. How long does the energy last? We worry about how to sustain it." There is a good chance that, like a battery, a team will run down after a period of time and will need recharging. This means that a mechanism ought to be in place to address the needs of teams during and after the first year back in the school.

Questions raised about the training and effectiveness of teams cut to the core of professional development itself. Is even team building up to the task of improving the ways in which teachers go about their work? Despite years of in-service activities, school improvement still founders and sometimes seems aimless. One group of researchers who studied in-service programs concluded, "Even with extended and intensive support it was difficult for teachers to change their practices" ("Findings on Learning," 1992, p. 7). The goals of the in-service programs in this study were to help teachers to improve their knowledge of subject matter, revise their thinking about their role in the classroom, and learn to manage substantially different teaching techniques. The research was conducted under the auspices of the Teacher Education and Learning to Teach Study of the National Center for Research on Teacher Learning at Michigan State University.

Fullan (1992a) offers a view that is less than sanguine when he speaks of the interrelatedness of staff development, implementation of innovations, and student outcomes, which he says require such a sophisticated, persistent effort to coordinate that success is seldom attained. "Any success that does occur," he says, "is unlikely to be sustained beyond the tenure or energy of the main initiators" (p. 100).

10

Team building in the long run

Team building for school change is still a curiosity. It exists on a modest scale, sustained largely by outside funds. If, however, team building is judged to be a promising vehicle for school change, there are many possibilities for making more extensive use of it. What might give team building a boost would be a revised perception of the role of professional development in bringing about school change. Until now, professional development has too often failed to make enough difference in the education of children. It has been largely piecemeal, and what happens one time frequently has little or no connection with what happened the last time or with what will happen the next time.

In his arresting study of professional development through an examination of its impact on a single mathematics teacher, David K. Cohen (1991) shows how lack of perspective on the part of the teacher might have deluded her into thinking that her progress in handling a new approach had been greater than it actually was. The fault lay not with the well-meaning teacher, who had indeed made *some* progress, but with a system of professional development that was simply inadequate.

There is apt to be better teaching and improved learning when professional development is no longer viewed as a fragmented add-on to what teachers do. Instead, it should be regarded as a basic component in the professional life of the teacher, as ingrained as day-to-day instructional activities. Schools could benefit by becoming places where teachers are always learning formally and informally. "The priority at the district level should be to encourage systematic reflection about classroom experiences and collegial interaction *within individual*

146

schools," recommends a report to the Ford Foundation (Academy for Educational Development, 1985). "By building staff development into the operation of a school, the school staff could make better use of resources" (p. 45).

LESSONS FOR PROFESSIONAL DEVELOPMENT

Make no mistake: The in-service education of schoolteachers will not be easily improved. Money is scarce. Time is precious. Collegiality is spotty. Team building, however, is an approach that just might help lift in-service to a new level. Although team building has many obstacles to overcome, it nonetheless represents some underlying principles that could be made integral to professional development, whether or not the exact pattern of the academy is emulated. An emphasis on the following outcomes, usually associated with team building, might reshape professional development in ways likely to contribute to school change:

- Team spirit
- Process skills that enable teachers to interact in more constructive and productive ways
- The fostering of a more intellectual climate in the workplace
- Teachers seeing themselves as sources of knowledge for their peers and as researchers capable of generating new knowledge
- New relationships with business, foundations, and higher education that build a network of support for professional development
- Closer links between professional development and the needs of elementary and secondary school children

Team Spirit

Teachers see themselves essentially as independent practitioners who carry out their craft among other independent practitioners with whom they have limited contact. Imagine, if you will, a medical office building filled with dentists—one per office, each engaged in a separate practice and, by coincidence, under the same roof as fellow professionals who happen to be doing similar work. A lot of schools are not terribly different from this medical building.

The existence of teams in schools does not necessarily mean that teachers will share classes, but that is not a negative mark on team building. In most cases, it is unlikely that there will ever be more than one teacher at a time in a classroom. What is supposed to happen, though, in schools where teams flourish is that teachers share a sense of mission. This feeling can be engendered and reinforced through interaction and common experiences that enrich the educational practice of each person whether that person works alone or with others. Presumably, the vision that guides the collective mission will lead to better education for students in the school. An aim of getting members of the school community to interact is to imbue them with "a sense of team identification" so that they feel "that they are part of a larger unit" (Bradley, Kallick, & Regan, 1991, p. 86). Esprit de corps can translate into a commitment to contribute to the betterment of the larger enterprise.

No teacher in such a school should be confused about objectives. The ideal is that all members of the school community eventually subscribe to the vision and be willing and able to follow the steps for fulfilling it. Teachers in such settings know that they have colleagues to whom they can turn whenever they feel the need. Where there is team spirit and collegiality, no one should have to hesitate in seeking or rendering aid. What a difference from schools in which the mood of the individual practitioner reigns to the extent that few in the building take an interest in the work of others and there is no particular inclination to reach out to anyone to offer professional assistance.

Team spirit is very much related to the kind of bonding that most academies try to inculcate in teams. Anyone who has been a member of a successful sports team can recall the exhilarating sense of bonding that contributed to and resulted from that success. Where there is bonding, there is less psychological isolation. This bonding—this sort of team spirit—can nourish the professional self-renewal of teachers (James, 1991).

Process Skills

An outcome of functioning autonomously, as most teachers usually do, is that they may find it difficult to collaborate when expected to do so, even if only to make joint decisions about school policies. As there is no particular inducement to work in groups, it is not surprising that members of a school community don't cultivate group process skills. Increasingly, however, teachers are being called on to join teams or groups. This, for instance, is what shared decision making requires.

The kinds of group skills learned at an academy during team building can bring a qualitative change to the level of group work in a school, according to those who have attended academies. Such skills are learned experientially in the context of team building. A workshop that gives instruction in group process skills in the abstract would probably not be as successful as an experience in which members of teams must learn these skills in order for the team to function and to carry out its activities.

Intellectual Climate

Team building seeks to convert team members into people who behave in ways that will create a new ambiance in their school. They will talk about, read about, and be curious about the teaching and learning that affect students in the school. If the rest of the school community evinces no interest, the team will keep the conversation going among themselves in anticipation of the day when others will partake. In such a setting, Sykes (1990) envisions roles and tasks for teachers that "would serve to legitimate teachers' work outside of direct contact with students" and "contribute to the creation of a learning community" (p. 89) with a professional commitment to continuous growth.

The existence of a team in a school can potentially transform the intellectual milieu in that school. In other words, expecting the team to enhance the intellectual climate goes hand in hand with the philosophy of grounding professional development "in the mundane but very real details of teachers' daily work lives and in a form that provides the intellectual stimulation of a graduate seminar" (Goldenberg & Gallimore, 1991, pp. 69–70). The very nature of the team and its vision necessitates having certain consequential conversations. This doesn't mean that teams must be humorless about what they are doing. But the jocular moments can end up interspersed throughout discussions of significant matters that affect the school community. Seldom does the typical in-service effort have this result.

A math consultant for the San Francisco Unified School District laments the orientation of professional development toward specific programs rather than toward doing more to support simple dialogue among teachers (Olivo, 1991). Little (1989) points out that the encapsulation of professional development in formal programs detracts from the number and quality of informal learning opportunities that occur naturally during the working day.

The sort of professional climate that James (1991) concluded was fostered through faculty renewal in the 33 nonpublic schools that he studied resembles what team building strives to instill. In such circumstances, professional development "embraces the entire life of the school as a learning community" (p. 8), and "schools are able to influence the ways people relate to one another so that they take professional development seriously at all times" (p. 17). In the schools that were part of his study, this entailed newsletters and magazines that were produced and circulated, discussions at faculty meetings, notices on bulletin boards, study groups, breakfast gatherings, potluck dinners, and workshops to investigate educational issues.

Sources of Knowledge

What can be sought through team building is the formation of a network of individuals within a school building who become sources of knowledge for one another. It may even be that several teams that operate simultaneously in the same school serve this function. Right now, those who work in a school seldom collaborate in this way to help spread knowledge among themselves. Rather than arising from the teachers themselves, knowledge, like rain, more typically descends on the school from ethereal heights. The official knowledge base for teaching, say Cochran-Smith and Lytle (1992), is limited "to what academics have chosen to study and write about" (p. 300). As matters now stand, "the structure of many public schools inhibits knowledge-based teaching practice" (Abdal-Haqq, 1991, p. 1), and as a result, student learning may be inhibited.

This situation is frequently perpetuated by professional development in which in-service advice givers are people who have never before seen the teachers who compose their audience and who know nothing about their individual strengths and weaknesses (Eisner, 1992). It is unimaginative to assume that those who work in a school must turn to outsiders whenever they feel a need for new information. Schools will be more effective when more of the information that practitioners want to know is available from colleagues who work in their midst. The National Association of Secondary School Principals (1991) puts it this way:

> Traditional inservice delivery cannot keep up with all that school staff members need to know. There are not enough inservice days to "cover" all the material. An individualized program recognizes that theoretical and practical knowledge are more effective when vested in individuals who then work in teams and address problems and needs as they arise. (p. 1)

It might be possible that those within the school—people who know each other—could, in part, provide some of the knowledge that until now has been obtained only from the outside. The school community could draw on its own strengths. The notion of training the trainer has much in common with team building. A cadre, or team, of teachers exposed to ideas and trained in how to present those ideas to others becomes the bedrock on which restructuring of one sort or another may be based. In Richmond County, Georgia, the consolidated city-county school district created a professional development model that called for cadres to provide service to their colleagues (Murphy, 1991).

There are numerous possibilities for members of the school community in such a building: They might actually be consultants to one another, they might be active researchers, they could meet in study groups to discuss pedagogy or subject matter, and they would almost certainly collaborate on curriculum development.

Research by teachers can serve a variety of purposes. What is learned by teachers through practice can advance change because of the effect of the findings on future practice. Known as action research, this approach can promote the professional growth of classroom teachers. Generating new knowledge can make teachers better informed and more confident. The goal is not to convert schoolteachers into school-building versions of college professors. Rather, it is to foster a scholarly milieu in the schools, enriching an atmosphere in which professional growth is appropriate and important to the life of the school. If practice improves as a result, students are the winners.

Institutional support for action research both reflects and contributes to its recognition as a legitimate pursuit by teachers. The Harvard Educators' Forum, operating out of the university's Graduate School of Education, holds regular gatherings for teachers in elementary and secondary schools as well as for administrators, university faculty, and parents who are interested in action research or in merely discussing school improvement. Also, there are now programs such as the Teacher Research Institute to establish English teachers in secondary schools as authentic makers of knowledge. The institute is sponsored by the National Research Center on Literature Teaching and Learning at the State University of New York at Albany.

Study groups, too, can thrive in schools. Members of the school community might gather periodically in small groups to explore topics of mutual interest. One elementary school with which I am familiar has such meetings from 3:30 to 5:00 two afternoons a month. One group studies and discusses cooperative learning, another delves into mathematics, and yet another focuses on writing. Such ongoing discussions about the kind of work that is at the heart of schooling cannot help but enrich the professional community in the building.

Furthermore, schools where teachers have a role in generating knowledge are apt to be places where student teachers and interns best acquire the attitudes that will allow them to blossom into creative teachers with critical perspectives. Cochran-Smith (1991) writes of learning to teach against the grain. She has in mind the idea of placing novices in the company of experienced teachers who are engaged in the very sorts of activities described in these pages.

All of this is not to say that members of the school community ought no longer turn for knowledge to authorities outside the school. Outsiders, including practitioners from other schools, can contribute in many ways and should be called on whenever appropriate. Continued access to outside sources of knowledge, especially university-based scholars, enriches the curriculum work of teachers in a school and connects their work to external expertise and authority (Sykes, 1990).

New Relationships

Outside partnerships can be of considerable value to team building. Business, foundations, and higher education all have resources and expertise to help set up academies for building teams and to provide continuing assistance to teams once they return to schools. In combination with school districts, state education agencies, public education funds, and academic disciplinary organizations, these partners can help connect team building to professional development. Furthermore, outside partners may frequently have a role in providing the facilities, personnel, resources, and amenities for academies, retreats and workshops, and programs for the school staff.

It is incumbent on the central administration of school districts to accept responsibility for forging relationships with these partners, because the districts have so much control over the outcomes of such ventures. School districts have assumed an increasingly prominent position as both providers and consumers of professional development services (Little, 1989). Although outside partners—business, foundations, and higher education—have much to offer, school districts themselves must have a commitment to change if team building or any other major new efforts in professional development are to have a substantial impact.

*

Business has taken a degree of interest in elementary and secondary schools that could not have been foreseen as recently as the early 1980s, when colleges and universities appeared to be the sole area of education for which corporations evinced any large-scale concern. Corporate support for the schools grew from $31 million to $264 million between 1980 and 1990, according to the Council for Aid to Education (1991). However, some companies that have become generous with the schools too often seem to be throwing around money without any clear idea of what might be done to help education most. Business is increasingly frustrated by the inability of its investments in the schools to bring about substantial improvement (Bailey, 1991).

Were business to identify team building as a primary vehicle for its educational philanthropy, there would then be a chance to focus on an area in which the corporations are particularly well suited to make a contribution—and not simply of a financial nature. For one thing, business generally knows more than the schools about team building. Businesspeople, along with experts from higher education, could play a leading role in planning and coordinating academies. The possibilities are illustrated by the three-day workshops that the human resources department of United Technologies' Pratt & Whitney division conducted for the Wells-Ogunquit school system in Maine. Many of the elements included in this program were the same as those that the company uses in the workshops it runs for its own employees. Leaders in the schools were identified, invited to the workshops, and then charged with going back into the schools and forming teams.

Recognition of the importance of professional development and the role that business might take is underscored by business itself. In trying to frame an agenda to guide corporations in their support of elementary and secondary schools, the Business Roundtable formulated and published what it called the *Essential Components of a Successful Education System* (n.d.). One of the nine components is a major emphasis on staff development.

*

Foundations and other philanthropic organizations can be catalysts for changing the tenor of professional development in schools. The Rockefeller Foundation, for instance, attempted through the academies that it sponsored to heighten the awareness of teams of teachers and principals so far as the needs of at-risk children are concerned and to equip the teams with enhanced abilities to respond to the students' needs. In part, this called for familiarizing the teams with the School Development Program created by James Comer of Yale University. A school following this program sets up a management team that comprises parents, teachers, administrators, and support staff. The management team works in conjunction with a mental health team, a parents' program, and outside service agencies. The social growth of students is promoted as a foundation for greater academic growth.

The federal government has applauded the move by business and foundations to get more involved with elementary and secondary schools. David Rockefeller, Jr., a philanthropist with a special interest in schoolteachers, worries, however, that what Washington would like is for the private sector to pay for a portion of the day-to-day operations of the schools. "The real question," Rockefeller (1992) says, "is not whether philanthropy should be called on to support research and innovation in education—both are signal functions of philanthropy's mission—but whether this support supplements or supplants the government's previously accepted role" (p. 371). He adds that President Bush's call for his America 2000 education package should not drown out the need for other fundamental reforms that the private sector might back, including "expanded professional development of our teaching force" (p. 371).

Professional development is an area that may have special appeal during the 1990s to foundation officers, who increasingly recognize that teachers are pivotal to school reform. There is some feeling that foundations have had their fill of demonstration projects in individual schools and that the search now is for systemwide approaches that can make a difference. In this connection, foundations are more reluctant to be the sole funders of projects and want to see others contributing as well—as school systems might well be expected to do for professional development ("Foundations Likely," 1991). Academies for team building jointly run by consortiums of school districts could prove increasingly attractive to funders.

*

Inevitably, institutions of higher education must forge new kinds of relationships with elementary and secondary education, helping to make professional development an ongoing mission and activity in the schools. No longer will it be sufficient for colleges and universities simply to prepare future teachers in settings scarcely connected to schools and then dispatch them to their new jobs, while washing their institutional hands of further involvement. Rather, there is a huge role for higher education to play in the schools—in both the preparation of new teachers and the continuing education of veteran teachers. Furthermore, this sort of involvement is predicated on the participation of departments in the university besides those in the college of education.

One of the best ways to imagine this function is embodied in a theme echoed repeatedly in this book: thinking of the school as a place where the learning of staff is as much a part of the mission as the learning of children. A college or university can be a partner and a resource to the schools in such arrangements. Not only would college students preparing to be teachers spend time in the schools, but so would their professors—who would work as mentors and colleagues to the school faculty.

A visit to a classroom in such a school showed me what could happen when a university math professor and a third-grade teacher joined forces for their mutual gain and—most important—for the benefit of the children. The students were sitting in a large, lopsided circle on the floor, discussing prime numbers:

"Prime numbers are the ones you can only find one way," one of the students, Adrienne, said.

"Those are the ones we've written in pink," said the professor, referring to a large chart. "What do we call a number that can be made in more than one way?"

"A composite number," Jason responded.

"So we call '14' a composite number," the professor said to the eight-year-olds.

"It's important to write about that in your journals," their teacher, sitting next to the professor, reminded the children. She asked that each student "adopt" the number that had been written next to his or her name and take the next five minutes to prepare to talk about that number.

This was a classroom in which the teacher believed that students had the potential to truly care about math. She said that she and the students benefited enormously from her colleagueship with the professor. For his part, the professor, who had a grant from the National Science Foundation for this work, was getting his initial exposure that semester to third graders and was trying to discover how much of what is usually not taught until the sixth grade could be introduced earlier.

Notions of schools of this sort have different names and slightly different concepts. The Holmes Group calls them professional development schools, the American Federation of Teachers calls them professional practice schools, and John L. Goodlad's Center for Educational Renewal calls them teaching schools. Whatever the name, the six principles set out by the Holmes Group for the organization of professional development schools are an appropriate starting point for any consideration of this new relationship between higher education and schools. The following are the six principles (The Holmes Group, 1990):

1. Teaching and learning for understanding. . . .
2. Creating a learning community. . . .
3. Teaching and learning for understanding for everybody's children. . . .
4. Continuing learning by teachers, teacher educators, and administrators. . . .
5. Thoughtful long-term inquiry into teaching and learning. . . .
6. Inventing a new institution. . . . (p. 7)

Students' Needs

Students' needs have for the most part dictated the agendas of the academies. The fallout from this trend could have a salutary influence on professional development generally. After all, why else are teachers employed if not to meet the educational needs of children? Yet, as obvious as the answer to this question may appear, professional development programs sometimes seem to exist apart from the needs of students.

This is not to say that everything about team building or any other venture into professional development can or should always put primary emphasis on students. Having teachers learn process skills, for instance, is somewhat distant from the principal instructional responsibilities of teachers. Ideally, however, there will usually be a rationale relevant to students even for the parts of team building that seem less connected to the world of students.

A poll of those who participated in academies for team building in Minnesota found that 32% felt that students got better instruction as a result of the experiences of their teachers and that 20% felt that students benefited from the positive climate that was cultivated in the school after the team attended an academy. On the other hand, 18% said that the program had little or no impact on students, and 14% were unsure of the effect on students (Minnesota Department of Education, 1992).

If team building diverges too far from the needs of students, it will be peripheral to the show being performed in the center ring. It will be little more than another sideshow, and education already has more than enough of those. This means that teams have a special responsibility not to lose sight of the reasons why they are singled out for the attention they receive. Team building must be called into question if it does not somehow add up to a sum that improves the education of students. The needs of students must ultimately justify what occurs in the name of team building, however indirect the road to that goal may be.

REFERENCES

Abdal-Haqq, I. (1991, September). Professional development schools and educational reform: Concepts and concerns. *ERIC Digest.*

Academy for Educational Development. (1985). *Teacher development in schools: A report to the Ford Foundation.* New York: Author.

Argyris, C. (1962). *Interpersonal competence and organizational effectiveness.* Homewood, IL: Dorsey Press.

Arhar, J., Johnston, J., & Markle, G. (1988). The effects of teaming and other collaborative arrangements. *Middle School Journal, 19*(4), 22–25.

Aschbacher, P. (1991). Humanitas: A thematic curriculum. *Educational Leadership, 49*(2), 16–19.

Asians far outstrip Americans in math, researcher shows. (1991, December 12). *Education Daily,* p. 1.

Bailey, A. (1991, May 7). Business failing to transform schools, study finds. *Chronicle of Philanthropy,* p. 12.

Barrett, M. (1990, November). The case for more school days. *The Atlantic,* pp. 78–106.

Barth, R. (1988). School: A community of leaders. In A. Lieberman (Ed.), *Building a professional culture in schools* (pp. 129–147). New York: Teachers College Press.

Barth, R. (1990). *Improving schools from within: Teachers, parents and principals can make a difference.* San Francisco: Jossey-Bass.

Barth, R. (1991). Restructuring schools: Some questions for teachers and principals. *Phi Delta Kappan, 73,* 123–128.

Basom, R., Jr., & Crandall, D. (1991). Implementing a redesign strategy: Lessons from educational change. *Educational Horizons, 69*(2), 78–82.

Bass, B. (1990). *Bass & Stogdill's handbook of leadership.* New York: Free Press.

Bellah, R., Madsen, R., Sullivan, W., Swidler, A., & Tipton, S. (1985). *Habits of the heart.* Berkeley, CA: University of California Press.

Bennett, J. (1991, October). Collegiality as "getting along." *AAHE Bulletin,* pp. 7–10.

Bennett, N., & Carre, C. (1991, November 8). No substitutes for a base of knowledge. *Times Education Supplement (London),* p. 14.

Bolmer, M. (1991). A teacher's total work time. *Educational Horizons, 69*(2), 68–71.

Bradley, M., Kallick, B., & Regan, H. (1991). *The staff development manager: A guide to professional growth.* Boston: Allyn and Bacon.

Business–Higher Education Forum. (1991). *Highlights of the summer 1991 meeting.* Washington, DC: Author.

California principals work together to meet future challenges. (1991, July 17). *Education Daily,* p. 6.

Carnegie Commission on Science, Technology and Government. (1991). *In the national interest.* New York: Author.

Carnegie Corporation. (1989). *Turning points.* New York: Author.

Carnegie Foundation for the Advancement of Teaching. (1990). *The condition of teaching.* Princeton, NJ: Author.

Carving out time for teacher renewal. (1991, February). *Catalyst,* p. 4.

Cherry, M. (1991, October). School ownership—The essential foundation of restructuring. *NASSP Bulletin,* pp. 33–39.

Cipra, B. (1992). *On the mathematical preparation of elementary school teachers.* Chicago: University of Chicago Press.

Coalition of Essential Schools. (1989, May). *HORACE.* Providence, RI: Author.

Coalition of Essential Schools. (n.d.[a]). *The common principles.* A two-sided handout listing the nine principles of the Coalition of Essential Schools. Providence, RI: Author.

Coalition of Essential Schools. (n.d.[b]). *The Trek: A year-long course of study.* Providence, RI: Author.

Cochran-Smith, M. (1991). Learning to teach against the grain. *Harvard Educational Review, 61,* 279–310.

Cochran-Smith, M., & Lytle, S. (1992). Communities for teacher research: Fringe or forefront? *American Journal of Education, 100,* 298–324.

Cohen, David. (1991, Fall). Revolution in one classroom (or, then again, was it?). *American Educator,* pp. 16–48.

Cohen, Deborah. (1991, September 25). Reality tempers "new futures" leaders' optimism. *Education Week,* p. 1.

Cohen, R. (1992, May 16). Suzuki in Hungary: Team spirit soars. *New York Times,* p. 37.

Coleman, J. (1966). *Equality of educational opportunity.* Washington, DC: US Department of Health, Education and Welfare.

Council for Aid to Education. (1991, December). Corporate giving reaches $6 billion in 1990. *Education Support Today,* p. 1.

Cuban, L. (1988). A fundamental puzzle of school reform. *Phi Delta Kappan, 69,* 341–344.

Cushman, K. (1992, March/April). Time to craft lessons: A key to Asian student success. *The Harvard Education Letter,* pp. 4–5.

David, J. (1991). What it takes to restructure education. *Educational Leadership, 48*(8), 11–15.

Deal, T., & Peterson, K. (1990). *The principal's role in shaping school culture.* Washington, DC: US Department of Education.

Diegmueller, K. (1991, September 18). Teachers' strikes up 36% amid signs of growing tension. *Education Week,* p. 5.

Disciplining of principals scores badly. (1991, January 29). *Newsday,* p. 2.

Drucker, P. (1992, February 11). There's more than one kind of team. *Wall Street Journal,* p. 16.

Druckman, D., & Bjork, R. (Eds.). (1991). *In the mind's eye: Enhancing human performance.* Washington, DC: National Academy Press.

Education Commission of the States. (1989, August). *Clearinghouse notes.* Denver: Author.

Education Commission of the States. (1991). *Status of reform 1991: A report to the business-education policy forum.* Denver: Author.

Eisner, E. (1992). Educational reform and the ecology of schooling. *Teachers*

College Record, 93, 610–628.

Essential components of a successful education system. (n.d.). New York: Business Roundtable.

Farber, B. (1991). *Crisis in education: Stress and burnout in the American teacher.* San Francisco: Jossey-Bass.

Foster, A. (1991). When teachers initiate restructuring. *Educational Leadership, 48*(8), 27–30.

Foundations likely to fund systemwide plans, experts say. (1991, July 25). *Education Daily,* p. 1.

Friedman, I. (1991). High- and low-burnout schools: School culture aspects of teacher burnout. *Journal of Educational Research, 84,* 325–333.

Fullan, M. (1990). Staff development, innovation, and institutional development. In B. Joyce (Ed.), *Changing school culture through staff development* (pp. 3–25). Alexandria, VA: Association for Supervision and Curriculum Development.

Fullan, M. (1992a). *Successful school improvement: The implementation perspective and beyond.* Philadelphia: Open University Press.

Fullan, M. (1992b). Visions that blind. *Educational Leadership, 49*(5), 19–20.

Fullan, M., & Miles, M. (1992). Getting reform right: What works and what doesn't. *Phi Delta Kappan, 73,* 745–752.

Fullan, M., & Stiegelbauer, S. (1991). *The new meaning of educational change.* New York: Teachers College Press.

Gardner, J. (1984). *Excellence: Can we be equal and excellent too?* (rev. ed.). New York: W.W. Norton.

Gardner, J. (1990). *On leadership.* New York: Free Press.

Garmston, R. (1991). Staff developers as social architects. *Educational Leadership, 49*(3), 64–65.

Gatto, J. (1991, July 25). I may be a teacher, but I'm not an educator. *Wall Street Journal,* p. A8.

Geoghegan, T. (1992). *Which side are you on? Trying to be for labor when it's on its back.* New York: Farrar, Straus & Giroux.

Gideonse, H. (1990). Organizing schools to encourage teacher inquiry. In R. Elmore (Ed.), *Restructuring schools: The next generation of educational reform* (pp. 97–125). San Francisco: Jossey-Bass.

Goldenberg, C., & Gallimore, R. (1991). Changing teaching takes more than a one-shot workshop. *Educational Leadership, 49*(3), 69–72.

Goldman, J. (1992, January). When participatory management attracts no buyers. *The School Administrator,* p. 15.

Goodlad, J., & Anderson, R. (1959). *The nongraded elementary school.* New York: Harcourt, Brace & World.

Grumet, M. (1991). Dinner at Abigail's. In P. Barrett (Ed.), *Doubts & certainties: Working together to restructure schools* (pp. 107–118). Washington, DC: National Education Association.

Gutmann, A. (1987). *Democratic education.* Princeton, NJ: Princeton University Press.

Harper, S. (1991, March). *NEA Today,* p. 31.

Hart, A. (1990). Impacts of the school social unit on teacher authority. *American Educational Research Journal, 27,* 503–532.

Hawley, W. (1978). Horses before carts: Developing adaptive schools and the limits of innovation. In D. Mann (Ed.), *Making change happen* (pp. 224–260). New York: Teachers College Press.

Heyns, B. (1978). *Summer learning and the effects of schooling.* New York: Academic Press.

Hill, P., & Bonan, J. (1991). *Decentralization and accountability in public education.* Santa Monica, CA: RAND Corporation.

Hill, P., Foster, G., & Gendler, T. (1990). *High schools with character.* Santa Monica, CA: RAND Corporation.

The Holmes Group. (1990). *Tomorrow's schools: Principles for the design of professional development schools.* East Lansing, MI: Author.

Holzman, M., & Tewel, K. (1992). The San Diego Panasonic partnership: A case study in restructuring. *Teachers College Record, 93,* 488–499.

Iowa State Education Association. (n.d.). *Time for a change.* Des Moines: Author.

James, T. (1991). *Adventurous teachers, excellent schools.* Stamford, CT: Charles E. Culpeper Foundation.

Jehl, J., & Payzant, T. (1992). Philanthropy and public school reform: A view from San Diego. *Teachers College Record, 93,* 472–487.

Joyce, B., Bennett, B., & Rolheiser-Bennett, C. (1990). The self-educating teacher: Empowering teachers through research. In B. Joyce (Ed.), *Changing school culture through staff development* (pp. 26–40). Alexandria, VA: Association for Supervision and Curriculum Development.

Lacoutre, J. (1992). *DeGaulle: The ruler 1945–1970.* New York: W.W. Norton.

Larson, C., & LaFasto, F. (1989). *TeamWork.* Newbury Park, CA: Sage Publications.

Leithwood, K. (1990). The principal's role in teacher development. In B. Joyce (Ed.), *Changing school culture through staff development* (pp. 71–90). Alexandria, VA: Association for Supervision and Curriculum Development.

Leithwood, K. (1992). The move toward transformational leadership. *Educational Leadership, 49*(5), 8–12.

Levin, H. (1991). *Building school capacity for effective teacher empowerment: Applications to elementary schools with at-risk students.* New Brunswick, NJ: Consortium for Policy Research in Education, Rutgers University.

Levine, D. (1991). Creating effective schools: Findings and implications from research and practice. *Phi Delta Kappan, 7,* 389–393.

Levine, D., & Lezotte, L. (1990). *Unusually effective schools.* Madison, WI: National Center for Effective Schools Research and Development.

Lewis, A. (1991). *Gaining ground.* New York: Edna McConnell Clark Foundation.

Lewis, A. (1992, May). Making time for reform. *High Strides,* p. 3.

Lieberman, A., Darling-Hammond, L., & Zuckerman, D. (1991). *Early lessons in restructuring schools.* New York: National Center for Restructuring Education, Schools, and Teaching/Teachers College.

Lieberman, A., & McLaughlin, M. (1992). Networks for educational change: Powerful and problematic. *Phi Delta Kappan, 73,* 673–677.

Lightfoot, S. (1983). *The good high school.* New York: Basic Books.

Lindquist, K., & Mauriel, J. (1989). School-based management: Doomed to failure? *Education and Urban Society, 21,* 403–416.

Little, J. (1988). Assessing the prospects for teacher leadership. In A. Lieberman

(Ed.), *Building a professional culture in schools* (pp. 78–108). New York: Teachers College Press.

Little, J. (1989). District policy choices and teachers' professional development opportunities. *Educational Evaluation and Policy Analysis, 11,* 165–178.

Little, J., & Bird, T. (1984). *Report on a pilot study of school-level collegial teaming.* San Francisco: Far West Laboratory for Educational Research and Development.

Lockwood, A. (1992, Spring). The defacto curriculum. *Focus on Change,* pp. 8–10.

Louis, K., and others. (1981). *Linking research and development with schools, perspectives on school improvement: A casebook for curriculum change.* Washington, DC: National Institute of Education.

Lublin, J. (1992, February 13). Trying to increase worker productivity, more employers alter management style. *Wall Street Journal,* p. B1.

Maeroff, G. (1988). *The empowerment of teachers.* New York: Teachers College Press.

Maeroff, G. (1991). *Voices from the classroom: Exceptional teachers speak.* Washington, DC: National Foundation for the Improvement of Education.

Making time to make change. (1990, Fall). *Changing Minds,* pp. 1–4.

Mann, D. (1987). The politics of training teachers in schools. In D. Mann (Ed.), *Making change happen?* (pp. 3–18). New York: Teachers College Press.

Mansnerus, L. (1992, August 2). Mediocrity in the classroom. *New York Times,* p. 22.

Margolis, H. (1991, October). Understanding, facing resistance to change. *NASSP Bulletin,* pp. 1–8.

Meier, D. (1991). Choice can save public education. *The Nation, 252*(8), 253.

Meier, D. (1992). Reinventing teaching. *Teachers College Record, 93,* 594–609.

Michigan Academy. (1992). *Module summaries for the 1992 School Leadership Academy.* College of Education, Michigan State University.

Miles, M., & Louis, K. (1990). Mustering the will and skill for change. *Educational Leadership, 47*(8), 57–61.

Miller, E. (1992, March/April). Breaking the tyranny of the schedule. *The Harvard Education Letter,* p. 8.

Minnesota Department of Education. (1992). *Minnesota educational effectiveness program evaluation report.* St. Paul: Author.

Minnesota Department of Education. (1991). *Minnesota educational effectiveness program: Progress and evaluation report.* St. Paul: Author.

Mitchell, P. (1990). *Report on the evaluation of the Panasonic Foundation school improvement program.* Internal report to the Panasonic Foundation.

Murphy, C. (1991). Lessons from a journey into change. *Educational Leadership, 48*(8), 63–67.

Mutchler, S., & Duttweiler, P. (n.d.). *Implementing shared decision making in school-based management: Barriers to changing traditional behavior.* Austin, TX: Southwest Educational Development Laboratory.

Mydans, S. (1991, June 16). Bullets and crayons: children learn of 90's. *New York Times,* p. 14.

National Association of Secondary School Principals. (1991, June). Individual staff development for school renewal [Special issue]. *The Practitioner.*

National Center for Research on Teacher Learning. (1992). *Findings on learning to teach*. East Lansing, MI: Author.

National Commission for the Principalship. (1990). *Principals for our changing schools*. Fairfax, VA: Author.

New Mexico Academy. (1991). *New Mexico academy for school leaders: Summer program components*. Albuquerque: University of New Mexico, College of Education.

New Mexico Academy. (n.d.). *New Mexico academy for school leaders: 1991–92 proposal*. Albuquerque: University of New Mexico, College of Education.

Nickle, M., Flynt, F., Poynter, S., & Rees, J., Jr (1990). Does it make a difference if you change the structure? School-within-a-school. *Phi Delta Kappan, 72,* 148–152.

Noble, K. (1991, July 25). Togo's president bowing to change. *New York Times,* p. A6.

Nordhaus, M. (1990, September 12). *Preliminary report on summer session, 1990 academy*. Albuquerque: University of New Mexico, College of Education.

Nordhaus, M. (1991a). *Let there be change in the schools and let it begin with me*. Albuquerque: University of New Mexico, College of Education.

Nordhaus, M. (1991b, October 15). *1991 New Mexico academy for school leaders: Interim report*. An internal memorandum.

Oakes, J., & Lipton, M. (1992). Detracking schools: Early lessons from the field. *Phi Delta Kappan, 73,* 448–454.

Olivo, P. (1991, February). Teacher professionalism: Establishing a vision. *Angles,* p. 1.

O'Neil, J. (1991, December). National push for school reform, accountability to influence education's future agenda. *ASCD Update,* p. 3.

Palmer, P. (1992, March/April). Divided no more. *Change,* pp. 10–17.

Pauly, E. (1991). *The classroom crucible*. New York: Basic Books.

Pennell, A., & Alexander, D. (1991). *The management of change in the primary school*. New York: Falmer Press.

Peterson, D., & Hillkirk, J. (1991). *A better idea: Redefining the way Americans work*. Boston: Houghton Mifflin.

Peterson, K. (1991). The new politics of the principalship: School reform and change in Chicago. In S. Clements & A. Forsaith (Eds.), *Chicago school reform: National perspectives and local responses* (pp. 1–9). Washington, DC: Educational Excellence Network.

Putka, G. (1991, April 23). As fears are driven from the classroom, students start to learn. *Wall Street Journal,* p. 1.

Putting a priority on voice. (1991, November/December). *Doubts & Certainties,* pp. 1–3.

Rackliffe, G. (1991). The personal and the interpersonal: Neglected aspects of teacher leadership. In P. Barrett (Ed.), *Doubts & certainties: Working together to restructure schools* (pp. 163–178). Washington, DC: National Education Association.

RAND Corporation. (1991). *New and returning teachers in Indiana: Sources of supply*. Santa Monica, CA: Author.

Revised rules for principals. (1991, January 21). *New York Times,* p. B3.

Rockefeller, D., Jr. (1992). America 2000 and philanthropy's education agenda.

Teachers College Record, 93, 370–375.

Rutter, M. (1979). *15,000 hours.* Cambridge: Harvard University Press.

Sarason, S. (1982). *The culture of the school and the problem of change* (2d ed.). Boston: Allyn & Bacon.

Sarason, S. (1990). *The predictable failure of educational reform.* San Franciso: Jossey-Bass.

Sato, N., & McLaughlin, M. (1992). Context matters: Teaching in Japan and in the United States. *Phi Delta Kappan, 73,* 359–365.

Schlechty, P. (1990). *Schools for the 21st century.* San Francisco: Jossey-Bass.

Schlechty, P., & Cole, B. (1991). Creating a system that supports change. *Educational Horizons, 69*(2), 78–82.

Schmoker, M. (1992, May 13). What schools can learn from Toyota of America. *Education Week,* p. 23.

Schön, D. (1991). *The reflective turn.* New York: Teachers College Press.

Senge, P. (1990). *The fifth discipline.* New York: Doubleday Currency.

Sergiovanni, T. (1992). Why we should see substitutes for leadership. *Educational Leadership, 49*(5), 41–45.

Shanker, A. (1990). Staff development and the restructured school. In B. Joyce (Ed.), *Changing school culture through staff development* (pp. 91–103). Alexandria, VA: Association for Supervision and Curriculum Development.

Shanker, A. (1991). Reflections on 40 years in the profession. In D. Burleson (Ed.), *Reflections: Personal essays by 33 distinguished educators* (pp. 324–339). Bloomington, IN: Phi Delta Kappa Educational Foundation.

Shaplin, J., & Olds, H., Jr. (Eds). (1964). *Team teaching.* New York: Harper & Row.

Shedd, J., & Bachrach, S. (1991). *Tangled hierarchies.* San Francisco: Jossey-Bass.

Sizer, T. (1984). *Horace's compromise.* Boston: Houghton Mifflin.

Smith, M., & O'Day, J. (1991). Systemic school reform. In S. Fuhrman & B. Malen (Eds.), *The politics of curriculum and testing* (pp. 233–267). New York: Falmer Press.

Smylie, M. (1992). Teacher participation in school decision making: Assessing willingness to participate. *Educational Evaluation and Policy Analysis, 14,* 53–66.

Sommerfeld, M. (1992, June 10). RJR Nabisco lays $30-million bet on "bottom up" reform strategy. *Education Week,* p. 1.

Stevenson, H., & Stigler, J. (1992). *The learning gap.* New York: Summit Books.

Stigler, J., & Stevenson, H. (1991, Spring). How Asian teachers polish each lesson to perfection. *American Educator,* p. 12.

Stokes, S. (Ed.). (1982). *School-based staff support teams.* Washington, DC: ERIC Clearinghouse on Handicapped and Gifted Children.

Strategies for preparing teachers for diversity. (1992, Summer). *WCER Highlights,* p. 7.

Sykes, G. (1990). Fostering teacher professionalism in schools. In R. F. Elmore (Ed.), *Restructuring schools: The next generation of educational reform* (pp. 59–96). San Francisco: Jossey-Bass.

Teachers' majors and assignments. (1991, April 17). *Education Week,* p. 16.

Tewel, K. (1991a, October). A case study in reform. *American School Board Journal,* pp. 30–33.

Tewel, K. (1991b). Breaking the scheduling straightjacket. *Clearinghouse, 65,* 105–109.

Thomson, S. (1991, October 16). Leadership revisited. *Education Week,* p. 32.

Three central principles. (1991, Winter). *Accelerated Schools,* pp. 10–11.

Thurow, L. (1992). *Head to head.* New York: Simon & Schuster.

Trump, J., & Georgiades, W. (1977, May). What happened and what did not happen in the model schools. *NASSP Bulletin,* pp. 72–79.

Trump, J., & Georgiades, W. (1978). *How to change your school.* Reston, VA: National Association of Secondary Schools.

Twenty percent in high schools found to carry weapons. (1991, October 11). *New York Times,* p. A13.

Tyack, D. (1991). Public school reform: Policy talk and instructional practice. *American Journal of Education, 100,* 1–19.

Walters, D. (1992, August 3). Employees own a growing share of company stock. *Christian Science Monitor,* p. 7.

Walters, L. (1992, February 25). New era for pioneering university. *Christian Science Monitor,* p. 14.

Wasley, P. (1991). *Teachers who lead: The rhetoric of reform and the realities of practice.* New York: Teachers College Press.

Watkins, J. (1990, November 29). *Change teams in restructuring schools: Critical friends in the fray.* Paper presented at the annual meeting of the American Anthropological Association, New Orleans, LA.

Watkins, J. (1992, May). *The Trek: Part I: Rationale, structure, and essential questions.* Providence, RI: Coalition of Essential Schools.

Watkins, J. (1992). Critical friends in the fray: An experiment in applying critical ethnography to school restructuring. In G. Hess, Jr. (Ed.), *Empowering teachers and parents: School restructuring through the eyes of anthropologists* (pp. 207–228). Westport, CT: Bergin & Garvey.

Weissglass, J. (1992, June 3). Changing the system means changing ourselves. *Education Week,* p. 36.

Wellins, R., Byham, W., & Wilson, J. (1991). *Empowered teams.* San Francisco: Jossey-Bass.

Wentworth, M. (1989, April). The dynamics of change: Understanding and achieving community. *Doubts & Certainties,* p. 1.

What are accelerated schools? (1991, Winter). *Accelerated Schools,* p. 1.

White, J. (1992, February 13). When employees own big stake, it's a buy signal for investors. *Wall Street Journal,* p. 1.

Wiggins, G. (1990, June). Finding time. *Basic Education,* pp. 4–7.

Willrich, M. (1991, May). Class inaction: How 3,000 overpaid administrators stymie DC school reform. *Washington Monthly,* pp. 24–29.

Wilson, B., & Corcoran, T. (1988). *Successful secondary schools.* New York: Falmer Press.

Zaltman, G., & Duncan, R. (1977). *Strategies for planned change.* New York: John Wiley & Son.

INDEX

Abdal-Haqq, I., 150
Academies: attributes of, 16–17;
  commuter, 50, 70–72; examples
  of, 20–27; homework in, 50–51;
  origin, 1; part-time participants,
  70; purpose, 7; residential, 50,
  51, 70–72; schedule, 52; volun-
  tary participation in, 16, 41–42
Accelerated schools, 18, 20, 26–27,
  29, 43, 54, 115, 143
Administrators; support from, 29,
  92–97; on teams, 44
Alexander, D., 115
Alvarado, A., 92
American Federation of Teachers,
  18, 139
Anderson, R., 19
Annie E. Casey Foundation, 99, 102
Argyris, C., 113
Arhar, J., 9
Aschbacher, P., 39
Assessment, 3, 25; alternative, 23,
  37, 90; of change progress, 110;
  methods of, 2; norm-referenced,
  6; personality testing, 73
At-risk status, 16, 23, 27
Authority, 112; responsibilities in,
  87; sharing, 81, 84
Autonomy: giving up, 46, 48, 85;
  nurturing of, 88

Bachrach, S., 140
Bailey, A., 152
Barrett, M., 126, 127
Barriers to teams: budgets,
  137–139; continuity, 143–145;
  societal factors, 136–137;
  teacher knowledge and dedica-
  tion, 140–141; team function,
  141–143; unions, 139–140
Barth, R., 77, 91, 97
Basom, R., 140
Bass, B., 62, 65, 88

Bellah, R., 105
Bennett, B., 42
Bennett, J., 9
Bennett, N., 141
Bird, T., 9
Bjork, R., 142
Bolmer, M., 118
Bonan, J., 94
Bonding, 49, 66–79; beyond teams,
  75–78; teachers and principals,
  83; on teams, 28, 32
Bradley, M., 148
Budgets, 22; as barrier to teams,
  137–139; limitations of, 58; sig-
  nificance in change process, 47
Burnout, 106–107, 118
Byham, W., 15, 32

California Achievement Council
  (TEAMS II), 18, 30, 31, 110
Carnegie Commission on Science,
  Technology and Government, 18
Carnegie Council on Adolescent
  Development, 23
Carre, C., 141
Carroll, J., 131
Change: achieving, 80; agents, 14,
  57, 61, 94, 100; assistance for, 9;
  bottom-up approach to, 17;
  commitment to, 40; depen-
  dence on teachers, 9; difficulty
  of, 5–6; external, 3–4; internal,
  4; lack of in teaching, 2; process
  of, 34, 55, 67; proselytizing for,
  102; rate of, 102; role of principal in, 81, 84, 85; scheduling
  for, 118–123; school, 1; in students, 2; systemic, 34, 35, 140;
  in teacher behavior, 13; top-
  down, 5, 80, 99; unilateral, 7–8
Cherry, M., 84
Chicago Schools, 96, 133, 137
Chicago, University of, 89, 90

ABOUT THE AUTHOR

GENE I. MAEROFF is a senior fellow at the Carnegie Foundation for the Advancement of Teaching in Princeton, New Jersey, a position he has held since 1986. Previously, he was on the staff of the New York Times, where he was national education correspondent. Among his books are *The School-Smart Parent* (Times Books/Random House, 1989; Henry Holt, 1990); *The Empowerment of Teachers: Overcoming the Crisis of Confidence* (Teachers College Press, 1988); *Don't Blame the Kids: The Trouble with America's Public Schools* (Carnegie Foundation for the Advancement of Teaching, 1983); *School and College: Partnerships in Education* (McGraw Hill, 1982); and *The Guide to Suburban Public Schools* (with Leonard Buder; Times Books, 1976). In 1992, he was the editor of *Sources of Inspiration: 15 Modern Religious Leaders* (Sheed & Ward). His articles have appeared in education journals such as the *Phi Delta Kappan* and *Education Week* and in general-interest publications such as the *New York Times Magazine* and *Town & Country*. His writing has been recognized with first-place awards in competitions sponsored by the Education Writers Association, the International Reading Association, and the American Association of University Professors. Maeroff is a member of the Author's Guild and an outfielder on a team that plays in the Central Jersey Over-50 Softball League. He is the father of Janine, Adam, and Rachel; the father-in-law of Michael and Laura; and the grandfather of Romy, Harrison, and Max, triplets who were born in 1992. He lives in Edison, New Jersey.

Board Game as you go thru
the school